Exploring Science
and Belief

Acknowledgments

I am indebted to Professors 'Sam' Berry and John Brooke for their helpful comments on parts of an earlier draft of this book; and to Dr John Martin, John Bausor and Adrian Brown for suggestions following their extensive reading of the text. I am particularly grateful to my wife, Ginny, for her perceptive remarks and help at all stages of the preparation.

Michael Poole, King's College, London

Exploring Science and Belief

MICHAEL POOLE

HENDRICKSON
PUBLISHERS

Exploring Science
and Belief

Hendrickson Publishers, Inc.
P 0. Box 3473
Peabody, Massachusetts 01961-3473

ISBN 978-1-59856-225-5

Original edition published in English under the title *User's Guide to Science and Belief* by Lion Hudson plc, Oxford, England. This edition published with permission.

First Hendrickson Publishers printing—October 2007

A catalogue record for this book is available from the British Library

Typeset in 12/13 Lapidary333
Printed and bound in China

Contents

Introduction

Is science the ultimate test of what to believe?
    Do its laws make belief in miracles impossible?
    Has Darwin's work ruled out the idea of a creating God?

You've got to start somewhere

Cogito ergo sum, 'I think, therefore I am'; that is about as close as you can get to certainty! It was the starting point for the French mathematician and philosopher Descartes as he looked for something that he thought he could be sure about. Because he could think, he (reasonably) assumed he existed! But do our thoughts make sense?

Rationality

Rationality is the assumption, or presupposition, that our thought processes do make sense and are basically reliable. It is central to all branches of study, otherwise writing and talking would just be squiggles and noises. You cannot even meaningfully discuss whether rationality is a valid assumption without committing yourself to the assumption that it is!

You've got to stop somewhere

You cannot question everything at once. Even the total sceptic has this problem since *everything* includes scepticism! One has to suspend disbelief on some issues to make progress on others. So, to avoid constantly saying 'if God exists', except in the section on evidence for God, I shall follow Professor John Hick and '… start from what is for the theist the conviction, for the agnostic the hypothesis, and for the atheist the delusion that God exists'.

Some scientists have religious beliefs...

'We do not have to choose between the God of the Bible and the God revealed in the pattern and structure of the physical world.'
REVD DR JOHN POLKINGHORNE (FORMERLY PROFESSOR OF
THEORETICAL PHYSICS)

'... we must ourselves be prepared and willing to make a reasoned presentation of our faith, especially to young scientists, who have all too often concluded that a serious faith in a personal God and objective pursuit of scientific truth are incompatible'.
PROFESSOR FRANCIS COLLINS (DIRECTOR, NATIONAL HUMAN GENOME
RESEARCH INSTITUTE)

'For many years I have believed that God is the great designer behind all nature... one can be both a scientist and a Christian.'
PROFESSOR SIR GHILLIAN PRANCE (SCIENTIFIC DIRECTOR, EDEN
PROJECT)

... some do not

'... religious belief is incompatible with science...'
PROFESSOR LEWIS WOLPERT (BIOLOGY AS APPLIED TO MEDICINE)

'... the beliefs of most popular religions... by scientific standards... are based on evidence so flimsy that only an act of blind faith can make them acceptable'.
DR FRANCIS CRICK (CO-DISCOVERER OF DNA'S STRUCTURE)

'... successful mind viruses [i.e. religions] will tend to be hard for their victims to detect'.
PROFESSOR RICHARD DAWKINS (BIOLOGICAL SCIENCES)

In order to do science some additional presuppositions have to be made. These basic beliefs cannot be proved by science but must be assumed if we are even to begin.

Intelligibility

Whereas rationality assumes we can make sense of and understand things, intelligibility assumes the world can be understood. Otherwise there is no basis for science.

Orderliness

The belief that nature is orderly, that it is **cosmos,**[*] not **chaos**, makes it worthwhile searching for patterns, describable in concise 'summary statements' called scientific laws.

Uniformity

The uniformity of nature expresses the assumption that, even though the world changes, the underlying laws of nature remain the same in time and space.

Worthwhileness

Without the presupposition that science is a worthwhile activity, people would not engage in it. But science, which can be used for good in medicine can also be used for power and control for military and other purposes. The resulting issues of ethics and values require a book to themselves and will only be touched upon here.

SOME QUESTIONS:

1. How did the universe develop?

2. Was it accidental or planned?

3. What will happen to it eventually?

4. Do we have any significance in it?

1 and 3 are questions which science can address.
2 and 4 are questions that may be raised by science, but which 'science cannot address'.

[*]Key terms are shown in **bold** in the text where they are introduced.

'The most incomprehensible thing about the universe is that it is comprehensible.'

Professor Albert Einstein

'There are some questions that science cannot currently answer, and some that science cannot address.'

Science in the National Curriculum for England (2006)

1. God's 'Two Books'

'There is a long tradition of likening nature to a book: thus God
wrote both the "Book" of scripture (revelation) and the "Book of
Nature".'

PROFESSOR GEOFFREY CANTOR

This view sees the 'Book of Nature' as the
'Book of God's Works', and the 'Book of
Scripture' as the 'Book of God's Words'.
Francis Bacon (1561–1626), to whom the
development of early modern scientific
thinking owes so much, expressed this
same thought; so did Michael Faraday
(1791–1867) and Galileo (1564–1642),
who wrote in 1615:

'. . . it being true that two truths cannot
contradict one another, it is the function of
wise expositors to seek out the true senses of
scriptural texts. These will unquestionably
accord with the physical conclusions which
manifest sense and necessary demonstrations
have previously made certain to us.'

*English
philosopher,
essayist and
statesman Sir
Francis Bacon.*

The 'Two Books' figure of speech has been used by scientists
and theologians alike. Charles Darwin prefaced his *The
Origin of Species* with one of Bacon's 'Two Book' passages:

'To conclude, therefore, let no man out of a weak conceit of
sobriety, or an ill-applied moderation, think or maintain, that
a man can search too far or be too well studied in the book of
God's word, or in the book of God's works; divinity or

philosophy; but rather let men endeavour an endless progress of proficence in both.'
FRANCIS BACON, *ADVANCEMENT OF LEARNING*

Revd Dr Frederick Temple, later Archbishop of Canterbury, used the metaphor in a sermon referred to on p. 100:

'The student of science... if he be a religious man, he believes that both books, the book of Nature and the book of Revelation, come alike from God, and that he has no more right to refuse to accept what he finds in the one than what he finds in the other. The two books are indeed on totally different subjects; the one may be called a treatise on physics and mathematics, the other a treatise on theology and morals. But they are both by the same Author.'

The metaphor of 'God's Two Books' makes a good place to start looking at issues of science and religion since it raises some important questions:

- How are these 'Two Books' to be read?

- In what languages are they written?

- How do they relate to each other?

- What are the strengths and weaknesses of the metaphor?

The 'Book of God's Works'

It seems obvious today that discovering something about our world involves conducting experiments. Do the speeds of falling bodies depend on their weights, as Aristotle taught? All we need do is to time them falling to find, air resistance apart, that they all fall at the same rate. But before modern science developed, people consulted ancient authorities such as Plato and Ptolemy, who speculated how they thought the world *should* be. Since circular motion seemed most perfect, it seemed that all planets and stars (themselves assumed perfect) must move in circles.

Some 400 years ago, Francis Bacon brought a new emphasis – that we must consult nature, rather than people like Aristotle. Aristotle said life was impossible at the equator, but sailors disproved this by bringing back people from the tropics. Science came to be seen as the objective collecting of facts from which, by 'the Scientific Method', general laws were produced (the inductive method). But there is no single 'Scientific Method'. There are many; and good fortune and lucky guesses also play their part.

Selective science

It is now accepted that scientists usually start with some idea of what they are looking for, otherwise data-collection would be endless! In experiments on falling objects, people disregard the object's colour or ownership. Consciously or unconsciously, they reject these factors as irrelevant. If these initial ideas are confirmed by their experiments and checked by others, and are expressible in generalizations leading to successful predictions, then the word 'theory' is attached to them. Examples include the theories of relativity, gravitation and evolution.

Opponents of evolution sometimes say, dismissively, that

The story of Heinrich Hertz – a cautionary tale

Professor James Clerk Maxwell developed his Electromagnetic Theory of Light in the 1860s (pp. 15, 34). Nearly a quarter of a century later Hertz discovered radio waves, and wondered if they travelled at the same speed as Maxwell's light waves.

In designing an experiment, Hertz naturally assumed radio waves would travel as fast on Mondays as on Tuesdays, in a blue room or a green one and in a large laboratory or a small one. So Hertz ignored data he considered irrelevant. But assumptions about relevance can mislead. He obtained different speeds for radio and light waves, opposite to what Maxwell's theory predicted. After Hertz's death it was realized that radio waves, reflected from the walls, interfered with his measurements. So the 'obviously irrelevant' size of the laboratory turned out to be very relevant!

it is 'just a theory', thereby confusing the word 'theory' with a detective's 'hunch'; rather than recognizing the robust and well-tested status of a scientific theory.

Science also involves interpreting what we 'read'; there are 'spectacles behind our eyes'. What we believe – and are looking for – can powerfully affect what we think we 'see'. Someone scanning a shelf for a book title may overlook it if the cover is blue, when they believed it was red. Furthermore, unwelcome data, which contradict a favourite theory, can easily be overlooked without intentional dishonesty. Consequently science is committed to public testability through peer review.

As to the language of the 'Book of God's Works', Galileo, in his book *The Assayer*, published in 1623, identified it as follows:

> *'Philosophy is written in this grand book, the universe, which stands continually open to our gaze. But the book cannot be understood unless one first learns to comprehend the language and read the letters in which it is composed. It is written in the language of mathematics...'*

Portrait, c.1570, of French theologian and reformer John Calvin.

The next chapter explores language in more detail.

The 'Book of God's Words'

The Bible is a collection of 66 literary documents, authored by some 40 different writers over 1,200–1,500 years and written in Hebrew, Greek and Aramaic. More than 30 different literary styles or genres can be distinguished, including poetry, proverbs, parables, prophecy, history, prayers, songs, paradoxes and personal and circular letters. It is important to recognize these literary genres for, as Galileo pointed out: '... in expounding the Bible if one were always to confine oneself to the unadorned grammatical meaning, one might fall into error… it would be necessary to assign to God feet, hands and eyes…'

John Calvin (1509–64), a French theologian during the Protestant Reformation, wrote a commentary on Psalm 136:7 about God 'who made the great lights', saying, 'The Holy Spirit had no intention to teach astronomy; and, in proposing instruction meant to be common to the simplest and most uneducated persons, he made use… of popular language…' We still use the language of appearances when we talk of 'sunrise' and 'sunset'.

The Bible refers to the created order, for example, in Psalms 8 and 19. But Galileo complained about people who tried to force science, in this case astronomy, out of the Bible. 'The intention of the Holy Ghost,' he quoted, 'is to teach us how one goes to heaven, not how heaven goes.' Furthermore, Psalm 93:1 compares the steadfastness of God to that of the world: 'The world is firmly established; it cannot be moved.' Some took this to mean that the Earth cannot orbit the Sun, but such passages must not be read like a scientific journal.

'Twentieth-century Western culture seems to me particularly inept at understanding and using figurative or symbolic literature. We are so accustomed to straightforward, matter-of-fact descriptive prose that we expect nearly all writing to be of that form…scientific writing has made an illegitimate claim of superiority over artistic literature.'
PROFESSOR HOWARD VAN TILL

To take a passage literally, if the passage was not intended that way, fails to treat the text carefully enough, although it is not always easy to distinguish what is intended literally from what is a literary device. Even those who claim to 'take the whole Bible literally' rarely do so. They recognize poetry and imagery in expressions such as 'broken-hearted' and 'the valleys… shout for joy and sing' (Psalm 65:13).

Two words encountered in discussions about how the Bible should be read are **exegesis** and **hermeneutics**.

'The material imagery has never been taken literally by anyone who had reached the stage when he could understand what "taking it literally" meant.'

Professor C.S. Lewis

Exegesis is the attempt to determine the author's meaning. It attends to literary genre, historical context and what the words and sentences meant in the language of the time, including cultural idioms. For example, whereas we associate emotions with the heart, in Old Testament times they were associated with the bowels. Someone once remarked that this would require very different Valentine cards!

The opposite of exegesis is **eisegesis** – reading into the text what is not there – parodied by the couplet: 'Wonderful things in the Bible I see, some put there by you; some put there by me.'

Hermeneutics normally covers all aspects of interpretation, including exegesis, but it may refer, more restrictively, to seeking the relevance of ancient texts for us today.

As with the 'Book of God's Works', readers do not approach the text with entirely open minds. They are influenced, perhaps uncritically, by their presuppositions. These in turn are affected by their culture, by what counts as common sense and rational. Interpretations sometimes

say more about the interpreter than the text. Studying the text in turn modifies these presuppositions, reshaping subsequent study. This two-way, circular process is repeated and referred to as the **hermeneutical circle**. The term is applicable to science as well.

The 'kinds' of Genesis

The effect of presuppositions is illustrated by a science and religion issue. The book of Genesis says that God created everything 'after its own kind'. This can be read simply as saying that God acts in an orderly manner: dogs breed puppies, lions breed lion-cubs and not snakes or bees.

But some people read the text through the 'scientific spectacles' of our own culture. They take 'kinds' to mean the modern scientific term 'species', which is a reproductively isolated population, or group of populations. They then feel obliged to try to defend the 'fixity of species' and oppose evolutionary theory. But such a position seems to arise more from what is read into the text than out of it. Eisegesis can conjure up imaginary enemies, like the shadow-boxer who creates hazy opponents and then attacks them.

James Clerk Maxwell (pp. 34, 87), when discussing the creation and the origin of light, gave some wise advice against trying to read changing scientific theories into the Bible:

> 'I should be very sorry if an interpretation founded on a most conjectural scientific hypothesis were to get fastened to the text in Genesis… The rate of change of scientific hypothesis is naturally much more rapid than that of Biblical interpretations, so that if an interpretation is founded on such a hypothesis, it may help to keep the hypothesis above ground long after it ought to be buried and forgotten.'

The Genesis Text

The creation narratives are a blend of prose and poetry known as 'elevated prose'. Clearly there is symbolism

'The interpreter's prior decision about the possibility or impossibility of miracle is bound to influence his conclusions about the historicity of the miracle stories even more than his literary analysis of the traditions.'

Professor Graham Stanton

'The biblical creation narratives must not be used as a scientific account. They are concerned with theological truths. This is not to impute inaccuracy, but to insist upon the purpose of the passages.'

Professor Sam Berry

*Adam and Eve.
Stained glass
from Gloucester
Cathedral,
England.*

present because one cannot identify a 'tree of the knowledge of good and evil' (Genesis 2:17). Apples are not mentioned; the confusion may have arisen because the same Latin word *malum* is used both for 'evil' and 'apple'. What the eating of the fruit seems to symbolize is some kind of Unilateral Declaration of Independence from God, expressing the desire to 'go it alone'. Certain passages interpret Adam and Eve simply as representatives of humanity. But there are others that represent them as two people, as does the New Testament. So how would this fit in with the evolutionary development of *homo sapiens?* Perhaps the puzzling story of Cain and Abel gives the smallest of clues. When God calls Cain to account for the murder of his brother Abel, Cain replies, 'I will be a restless wanderer on the earth, and whoever finds me will kill me' (Genesis 4:14). The only other people mentioned so far are Adam, Eve and Abel; so who are those whom Cain feared?

It is sometimes thought that the account of Adam and Eve starting at Genesis 2:4 contradicts the earlier account given in Genesis chapter one, because of the differences in sequence. This does not necessarily follow. The criticism assumes that the intention is to give chronological accounts. The second account can be seen like a television documentary that, after giving a panoramic view in chapter one, zooms in on one feature, humankind.

In his commentary on Genesis, Professor Gordon Wenham has pointed out that the first people to hear Genesis knew other creation stories from the Canaanite, Babylonian and Mesopotamian traditions. The stories involved gods at war; humans feeding the gods; battles between equal and opposite forces of good and evil; worship of the Sun and Moon; sea monsters to be overcome and lesser gods doing the job of creation. In one tradition the seventh, fourteenth, nineteenth, twenty-first and twenty-eighth days were seen as unlucky. Matter was considered evil and there was faith in human progress and betterment. In contrast, Genesis chapter one is 'a tract against the times', setting out to rebut each of these views.

Imago Dei

One issue raised by evolution is whether the 'lowly origins' of our animal ancestry contradict the grand picture of bearing God's likeness. We share 98.8 per cent of our DNA with chimpanzees. At a lower level, everything is composed of selections of the same 92 naturally occurring elements. The Bible puts our origins even lower, as 'dust'. Physically, it appears we are descended not from apes, but from a common ancestor, and are classified as belonging to the animal kingdom. But how is a human being defined? Distinctions have been based on brain capacity, toolmaking, language and burial practices. These are useful for working in specific sciences, although chimpanzees can make rudimentary tools and can learn American Sign Language. But the Bible distinguishes humans as made in 'the image of God'. This involves having a potential spiritual relationship with God, best described in personal terms, rather than in physical form or bodily ancestry. Christians believe that it is a relationship broken by sin but reparable through Christ's work of forgiveness on the cross. Whether Adam is viewed as an individual, as representing humankind, or as both, the message of alienation from, and potential restoration to, God is the same.[1]

The last of the four earlier questions concerns the strengths and weaknesses of the 'Two Books' metaphor. One strength is that it provides an expressive way of saying God speaks to humankind both through the Bible and through creation. As Galileo put it: '... nor is God any less excellently revealed in Nature's actions than in the sacred statements of the Bible. Perhaps this is what Tertullian [c.160–c.230] meant by these words: "We conclude that God is known first through Nature, and then again, more particularly, by doctrine; by Nature in His works, and by doctrine in His revealed word."'

Or in the words of the apostle Paul: 'Since the creation of the world God's invisible qualities – his eternal power and divine nature – have been clearly seen, being understood from what has been made, so that men are without excuse' (Romans 1:20).

A potential weakness of the metaphor is that the interpretive factor is not obvious. But no comparison is perfect, as the next chapter shows.

2. Watch Your Language!

How could you explain the colour 'red' to someone blind from birth? People sometimes criticize religion for 'talking about kings, judges, light and old men in the sky'. 'Why', they ask, 'cannot religion use the plain, straightforward language of science?' But just how plain is that?

'Words, words, words...' said Hamlet; but words are all we have. Science and religion often use them in special ways: People's 'work' in religion may refer to their actions, for which they are held accountable; 'work' in science is 'the product of force and distance moved in the direction of the force'; in non-specialist language, work is what some people try to avoid!

Context is also important and many jokes depend on using identical words in different contexts. A notice in a chemist's window reading, 'We dispense with accuracy', might be reassuring or alarming since the *double entendre* of 'dispense' means either something you *do with* (medicines), or something you *do without*.

Words also have to serve as the means for talking about what may be invisible, new or conceptually difficult. We then resort to the 'it-is-as-if' language of analogies, similes, metaphors and models. We use something familiar that seems to have a similar form ('isomorphism') to what is unfamiliar, hoping to understand it better. For example:

SIMILES
'God is like a father.'
'Electricity in a wire is like a current of water flowing in a pipe.'

METAPHORS
'God is a father.'
'An electric current is flowing round the circuit' ('like' is dropped).

'Current' and 'flowing' have become so familiar that we rarely stop to think where the comparison came from. But would comparing electricity to water in a pipe help someone who had no piped water supply?

Here are another two examples from science:

1. Comparing light with water waves helps understand why light bends (slightly) round corners.

2. A hydrogen atom can be compared to a miniature solar system.

Some analogies, like the electricity/water one and the 'billiard-ball model', that treats gas molecules as tiny, elastic balls constantly in collision, are particularly helpful and have been developed in detail. They are then termed models, although we are not talking about toy scale-models *of* trains, but models *for* electricity and *for* atoms.

A model is a systematically developed analogy between something familiar and what it is we are trying to understand.

But care is needed; it is all too easy to assume analogies hold in every respect. 'Like an understudy, it is never quite the same as the principal' and 'every comparison has a limp'. Although a model will have a key concept, for example, water flowing in a pipe, comparisons with other features may not hold. Although all water can be emptied from a pipe, not all electrons can be removed from a wire.

During World War II, British planes dropped strips of tinfoil, which had lengths that would resonate with German radar frequencies. This gave the impression of a bombing raid, luring fighters away from a real raid elsewhere. The deception was exposed by other radar stations operating at different frequencies, giving weak reflections from the tinfoil and strong echoes at all frequencies from genuine aircraft. Another problem for successful deception was that moving aircraft gave a Doppler shift to the radar waves – like the change in note of a siren when an ambulance passes – unlike the drifting tinfoil. So...

'*... against an omniscient controller, we have to make the decoy echoes move with the speed of aircraft, and reflect different frequencies in the same way. This is easiest done by making a glider of the same size as the bomber. Then if we allow the enemy controller to use sound and infrared detectors and other aids, we find that the only decoy which can mislead him into thinking that there is a British bomber flying through his defences is another British bomber flying through his defences.*'

PROFESSOR R.V. JONES

An Avro Lancaster bomber.

If in every respect an analogy were perfect, it would no longer be an analogy, but an *identity*.

Since analogies are not literal descriptions and have limitations, some people think they should be avoided.

'*People who recommend it [abandoning analogy completely] have not noticed that when they try to get rid of man-like, or as they are called, "anthropomorphic", images they merely succeed in substituting images of some other kind. "I don't believe in a personal God", says one, "but I do believe in a great spiritual force." What he has not noticed is that the word "force" has let in all sorts of images about winds and tides and electricity and gravitation. "I don't believe in a personal God", says another, "but I do believe we are all part of one great Being which moves and works through us all" — not noticing that he has merely exchanged the image of a fatherly and royal-looking man for the image of some widely extended gas or fluid. A girl I knew was*

'[Models] originate in a combination of analogy to the familiar and creative imagination in the invention of the new... such models are taken seriously but not literally. They are... partial and provisional ways of imagining what is not observable.'

Professor Ian Barbour

brought up by "higher thinking" parents to regard God as a perfect "substance"; in later life she realised that this had actually led her to think of Him as something like a vast tapioca pudding. (To make matters worse, she disliked tapioca.)'
PROFESSOR C. S. LEWIS

Model-making

An important criterion for the choice of a model is its likely fruitfulness in generating further insights. Models have:

• Positive features – ways in which the two are alike.

• Negative features – ways in which the two are unalike.

• Neutral features – ones that are neither obviously positive or negative.

'. . . as long as the model is under active consideration as an ingredient in an explanation, we do not know how far the comparison extends – it is precisely in its extension that the fruitfulness of the model may lie'.
PROFESSOR MARY HESSE

The possible extensibility of a model is illustrated by part of a humorous after-dinner speech:

'The head of an Oxford college. . . is often thought of as a figurehead. Now what is a figurehead? It is a colourful, decorative but somewhat wooden personality, well to the front, representing the ship to the outside world. But it might be said that a figurehead is also virtually useless, needs pushing from behind if ever it is going to move at all; and yet everyone admits that if a storm breaks, it is the figurehead who bears the worst of it.'

Models in science

The solar-system model for atoms depicts electrons circulating a nucleus, like planets round the sun.

POSITIVE FEATURES:

• The atom is mainly space.

• Most of the mass is concentrated in the nucleus.

NEGATIVE FEATURES:

• The nucleus does not shine like the sun.

• The forces are electrical, not gravitational.

This model was supported by research by Geiger and Marsden, who fired alpha-particles (positively-charged) at gold foil. Some passed through, but some bounced straight back. Professor Rutherford, a supervisor, said: 'It was quite the most incredible event that ever happened to me in my life… as if you had fired a 15-inch shell at a piece of tissue paper and it came back and hit you.' In 1911 he suggested the solar-system model, the 'Sun' being a positively-charged nucleus.

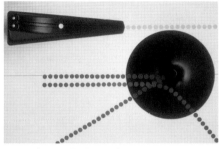

Apparatus for illustrating alpha-particle scattering.

But inspecting the negative features showed that this model was inconsistent with another well-accepted idea. Hertz had shown in 1887 that accelerating charges radiate energy and his work carried the consequence for Rutherford's model that all atoms should have collapsed. This negative feature was fruitful in prompting Niels Bohr to apply quantum theory to the electron energies. The solar-system model, however, is not helpful for advanced science and Professor R.B. Braithwaite gave the following caution:

> *'Hydrogen atoms are not solar systems; it is only useful to think of them as if they were such systems if one remembers all the time that they are not. The price of the employment of models is eternal vigilance.'*

Models in religion

It is not surprising that God-talk (theology) stretches language to its limit. Various models are used to try to convey different aspects of God's character. For example, he is compared to a (good) father/mother, a lover and a judge. The 'father' example has:

POSITIVE FEATURES

- We owe our being to God.

- God cares for us and disciplines us for our good.

NEGATIVE FEATURES

- Fathers may eventually need caring for by grown-up children.

- Some fathers get drunk and abuse their children.

The 'light' model is a good example of a systematically developed analogy used variously by Jews at Hanukkah, Christians at Christmas and Hindus, Sikhs and Jains at Divali. Light gives direction, warns of danger, promotes growth, enables communication, shows things as they really are, increases safety and provides enjoyment. Another powerful model is that of 'life', which is characterized by awareness and interaction. Christians believe that 'eternal life' speaks of the opportunity to experience God and interact with him through prayer.

Other pitfalls in using models

Models, by emphasizing different factors, may not be compatible with each other. For example:

- In religion, God is compared to both a loving father and a judge.

- In science, light is compared to both waves and particles.

A divine clock-maker?

Robert Boyle was a founder member of the Royal Society of London (1660). Reflecting on an intricate clock at Strasbourg, he suggested a clockmaker-model for God:

Positive features

• The universe, like the clock, can be seen as the product of design.

• God is separate from his creation, like the clockmaker and the clock. This countered the **pantheism** of an ancient Greek (600 BCE–CE 200) view of the world as a semi divine organism.

• The universe, like the clock, shows regular patterns of behaviour.

Negative features

• A clock cannot respond to its maker as we can respond to God.

• A clock, once made, does not need the clockmaker, except for occasional repairs and winding up.

Astronomical clock in the church of Notre Dame, Strasbourg.

'Impossible as it is to conceive of a "wavicle", a kind of hybrid between a wave and a particle, yet the two views must be held together.'

PROFESSOR R.L.F. BOYD

Metaphors and models, though generally helpful, can mislead. Sound needs a medium such as air, water or solids for transmission, so for a time scientists thought that light must also need a medium. This led to fruitless searches for a non-existent aether.

Failure to recognize the limitations of models led to the mechanistic model of a clock, encouraging deism. Contrary to Boyle's biblical beliefs, God came to be viewed as a creator whose work was finished and had retired from the scene, rather than as continuously involved in sustaining his creation.

Although in the above examples the misleading is accidental, models and metaphors can be used *about* religion as well as *within* religion, as instruments for persuasion; sometimes by comparing adult ideas about science with inadequate childish ones about religion.

'There is no need to be worried by facetious people who try to make the Christian hope of "Heaven" ridiculous by saying they do not want "to spend eternity playing harps". The answer to such people is that if they cannot understand books written for grown-ups, they should not talk about them. All the scriptural imagery (harps, crowns, gold, etcetera) is, of course, a merely symbolical attempt to express the inexpressible. Musical instruments are mentioned because for many people (not all) music is the thing known in the present life which most strongly suggests ecstasy and infinity. Crowns are mentioned to suggest the fact that those who are united with God in eternity share His splendour and power and joy. Gold is mentioned to suggest the timelessness of Heaven (gold does not rust) and the preciousness of it. People who take these symbols literally might as well think that when Christ told us to be like doves, He meant that we were to lay eggs.'
PROFESSOR C.S. LEWIS

Religion as a virus – a possible model?

Professor Richard Dawkins has described religions as 'mind viruses' (p. 7). The main features of viruses are that they spread and are often harmful. So a computer programme that, when introduced into our machine, duplicates itself and harms our hard drive, is termed a computer 'virus'. But what about religion? Certainly it spreads; this could be good *or* bad. Good things, like innocent laughter, can be caught as well as viruses. In the grim social climate of Britain in the eighteenth century, the Wesleyan revival transformed the lives of multitudes. It has been said that 'Religion is caught, not taught', and Charles Wesley (1707–88), the hymn-writer, likened the spread of Christianity to a blazing fire, longing 'that all might catch the flame'. Certainly it spread like wildfire but by terming religion a 'virus' Dawkins is implying it is harmful. It is all too easy to find examples of harmful religion – the Crusades, some tele-evangelists who line their own pockets, and terrorists who claim killing others is following God's will: nothing new here. Jesus warned his disciples that 'a time is coming when anyone who kills you will think he is offering a service to God' (John 16:2). He also said, 'My kingdom is not of this world. If it were, my servants would fight to prevent my arrest...' (John 18:36). He stressed the need for discernment about what people claimed to do 'in His name'; 'No good tree bears bad fruit, nor does a bad tree bear good fruit. Each tree is recognized by its own fruit' (Luke 6:43).

To claim religion is bad because evil things have been done in its name is a bad argument. It is like arguing that sex must be bad because evil deeds have been committed for sex. Both religion and sex involve powerful feelings and when they are misused the outcomes can be terrible. To try to persuade people that religion is bad for them one can list exclusively evil things, along with the weird and bizarre, and hope they

John and Charles Wesley preaching in the open air at Bristol, 1739. Wood engraving by Francis Arthur Fraser from The Sunday Magazine, *London, 1868.*

have not heard of schools and hospitals with religious foundations, or of acts of Christian love and costly forgiveness, like the following:

- Gordon Wilson, whose daughter Marie died in his arms from an IRA bomb in Enniskillen, forgave the IRA and pleaded for no reprisals from the Loyalists.

- Mrs Gee Walker, mother of Anthony, killed with an ice-axe in a racial attack, said 'Unforgiveness makes you a victim and why should I be a victim?'

- Nine-year-old Vietnamese girl Kim who in 1972 was seen on television running, naked and burning from Napalm, later cried out 'God, are you real?... Help me to learn how to forgive and how to love my enemies.' In 1996 she embraced the man responsible for co-ordinating the air attack on her village.

To believe that 'there is a God' is diagnosed by Richard Dawkins as having a 'mind virus' (p. 7). He then asserts, 'If you are the victim of one, the chances are that you won't know it, and may even vigorously deny it.' This seems to lead to a 'heads-I-win-tails-you-lose' stalemate. You can agree you have it, but if you 'vigorously deny it', someone, presumably with some privileged insight, will assure you that you have it but do not know it!

Is atheism a virus? To believe 'there is no God' could also be a 'mind virus' since no one possesses all truth. Presumably the same standards must apply, with the possibility of an atheist being a permanent, unknowing victim of delusion.

'Religion is a virus? I wish it could be spread that easily! Actually, that view shows a poor knowledge of the history of the human race. If religion is an illness, then most people, in most cultures, through most of human history, have been sick!'
PROFESSOR NANCEY MURPHY

'Religion is a virus' is a catchy phrase and people who dislike religion may adopt it. This leads to the question of whether the phrase 'Religion is a virus' is itself a virus that says 'Duplicate me'?

'Transposition'

An imaginative treatment of the limitations of language occurs in C.S. Lewis' essay 'Transposition'. He addresses the criticism that 'religious language and imagery... contains nothing that has not been borrowed from Nature'; so is there anything else? He compares 'poorer systems' and 'richer systems' on Earth, using examples from music and art where the same symbols have to serve for both simple and more complex ideas. Then he extends the comparison to earthly and heavenly things. Here is a flavour of his argument:

> 'If the richer system is to be represented in the poorer at all, this can only be by giving each element in the poorer system more than one meaning... If you are making a piano version of a piece originally scored for an orchestra, then the same piano notes which represent flutes in one passage must also represent violins in another...
>
> 'The piano version means one thing to the musician who knows the original orchestral score and another thing to the man who hears it simply as a piano piece. But the second man would be at an even greater disadvantage if he had never heard any instrument but a piano and even doubted the existence of other instruments.'

In this book many analogies, similes, metaphors and models are used. They need to be kept under review for their positive, negative and neutral features, to decide whether they are valid or inappropriate. They are useful tools for explaining things, which is the subject of the next chapter.

3. Explaining Explanations

To explain something is to make it plain. There are different ways of doing this. Here are three main types of explanation a parent might use to explain the concept of a 'kettle' to a child. They correspond to the questions 'What?', 'How?', and 'Why?', but only roughly in the latter case, since 'Why?' is ambiguous.

WHAT IS A KETTLE?

A container for heating up water. Called an **interpretive** explanation, it clarifies what the word kettle means.

HOW IS IT MADE UP?

This needs a **descriptive** explanation detailing (usually) a handle, a spout, a lid and perhaps an electric heater.

WHY DOES IT MAKE WATER HOT?

This requires a **reason-giving** explanation. Electricity 'flowing' through the heating element heats the water. But other reason-giving explanations, answering different 'why' questions, are possible:

Imagine a kettle of water boiling in a laboratory. A technician asks the student, 'Why is that kettle of water boiling over there?' The 'Why?', on paper, is ambiguous; but if spoken, the tone of voice and context normally give clues. One answer is, 'Because energy is transferred, raising the temperature of the water until its vapour pressure equals that of the surrounding atmosphere, when it boils' (reason-giving [scientific] explanation). Another answer could be 'Because I want a cup of tea', (reason-giving [motives] explanation). But the reply 'That wasn't what I was asking! I want an explanation (reason-giving [obligation]) of why you're disobeying rules that forbid drinking in laboratories' indicates why the first two types of explanations were not envisaged. A **type-error** is committed if an explanation of a different type is given from what is required.

These three types of explanation are not in competition, but are *compatible*. It would be nonsense to deny the agency and purpose of the disobedient student because a scientific explanation was available. Herein lies the oddity of the statement, 'People used to think God created the world; but now we know it was a Big Bang.' The two are not logical alternatives, whether or not one believes in God. One is an *act*; the other is a *process*. Understanding how the world came into being does not invalidate the idea of a creator. It would be rather like claiming that a physical explanation of an invention denies an inventor. The common tendency to think one type of explanation can oust another of a different type has been compared to one noisy fledgling in a nest trying to evict others that have an equal and independent right to be there. Perhaps any type of explanation relieves our frustration with the unexplained, so other types are not sought and may even be denied.

Scientific explanations are not the only types of explanations, nor necessarily the best. A scientific explanation of a person's body-chemistry is best if the objective is to create a healing medicine, but it is inappropriate if the knowledge required is for starting a friendship.

Science and religion are largely concerned with different types of explanations. Scientific ones aim at showing that single events, such as a falling object, conform to general patterns, described by scientific laws like the law of gravity. Such an event is scientifically explained if, knowing the relevant laws and initial conditions, we can predict it. Even with this knowledge, however, prediction may be impossible on account of complexity (for example, predicting the weather, six months from now). Chaos theory – better-named **complexity theory** – deals with events where

Einstein was once asked if he thought everything could be put in scientific terms and he replied: 'Yes, that is conceivable, but it would make no sense. It would be as if one were to reproduce Beethoven's Ninth Symphony in the form of an air pressure curve.'

minute changes in initial conditions lead to vastly different outcomes. A meteorologist, Edward Lorenz, re-ran a weather forecasting programme leaving out lower places of decimals and, surprisingly, obtained a very different result. His question, 'Does the flap of a butterfly's wings in Brazil set off a tornado in Texas?' led to such behaviour being dubbed the 'butterfly effect'. Nevertheless, scientists seek physical answers to physical questions; but explanations of ultimate purpose in the universe are outside the scope of science.

Does Science Need God?

In scientific writings long ago, 'First Causes' were sometimes mentioned. Secondary causes were the physical causes studied in science (called **Natural Philosophy** before the

word 'scientist' was coined in 1834). 'There was a Big Bang' is a modern secondary cause explanation for our universe; 'God brought the universe into being' would be a first cause explanation. Sir Isaac Newton (1642–1727) once wrote to a Dr Bentley saying, 'When I wrote my Treatise (*Principia Mathematica*) about our System, I had an Eye upon such Principles as might work with considering Men, for the Belief of a Deity, and nothing can rejoice me more than to find it useful for that Purpose.'

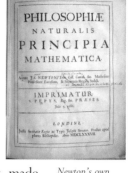

Newton's own copy of the Principia, *showing his handwriting.*

Mention of God in scientific writings is rarely made nowadays since science only deals with secondary causes. This practice enables those of various faiths, and none, to work together on a common enterprise. It does not mean that modern scientists do not believe in God: some do, some do not (p. 7). The science of a television set can be studied without mentioning its inventors. Such omissions offer no snub to the inventors Zworykin, or Baird – or God!

Pushing God out?

Many years ago, some theologians said they thought God kept the planets in orbit, but then they were told it was gravity. Believing God was being pushed out, they tried to plug the gaps in scientific explanations with religious ones about God. But there is no *necessary* contradiction in believing both that there are scientific explanations of how it happens and that it is God's activity – the subject of theology, or 'God-talk'. The confusion, however, meant that as the mechanisms of the universe became better understood, God's part in it inevitably shrank! This classic case of an explanatory type-error is so common that Professor C.A. Coulson gave it a name: the 'God-of-the-gaps'. Writing from a Christian perspective he regarded the position as unbiblical and unscientific:

'If He is in nature at all, He must be there right from the start, and all the way through it.'

'I believe that the limits of science are only those which are presented by the following words: if a question about nature can be posed in scientific terms, then ultimately it will be susceptible of a scientific answer. Science does not lead us through its own country to the boundary of the scientifically unknown, explaining to us that this is where we have to deal with God. When we come to the scientifically unknown, our correct policy is not to rejoice because we have found God: it is to become better scientists.'

Two compatible accounts, theological and scientific (Maxwell's equations for his electromagnetic theory of light).

Some who hold a 'God-of-the-gaps' position also believe certain areas are 'fenced off' to science because they are God's working, and they may see science as threatening. But this does not follow. Others, though not believing in God, nevertheless see 'God' used as a stop-gap, awaiting scientific explanations.

And God said,

$$\frac{1}{r^2}\frac{\partial}{\partial r}(r^2 D_r) + \frac{1}{r\sin\theta}\frac{\partial}{\partial\theta}(D_\theta\sin\theta) + \frac{1}{r\sin\theta}\frac{\partial D_\phi}{\partial\phi} = 4\pi\rho,$$

$$\frac{1}{r^2}\frac{\partial}{\partial r}(r^2 B_r) + \frac{1}{r\sin\theta}\frac{\partial}{\partial\theta}(B_\theta\sin\theta) + \frac{1}{r\sin\theta}\frac{\partial B_\phi}{\partial\phi} = 0;$$

$$\frac{1}{r\sin\theta}\left[\frac{\partial}{\partial\theta}(E_\phi\sin\theta) - \frac{\partial E_\theta}{\partial\phi}\right] = -\frac{1}{c}\frac{\partial B_r}{\partial t},$$

$$\frac{1}{r}\left[\frac{1}{\sin\theta}\frac{\partial E_r}{\partial\phi} - \frac{\partial}{\partial r}(rE_\phi)\right] = -\frac{1}{c}\frac{\partial B_\theta}{\partial t},$$

$$\frac{1}{r}\left[\frac{\partial}{\partial r}(rE_\theta) - \frac{\partial E_r}{\partial\theta}\right] = -\frac{1}{c}\frac{\partial B_\phi}{\partial t};$$

$$\frac{1}{r\sin\theta}\left[\frac{\partial}{\partial\theta}(H_\phi\sin\theta) - \frac{\partial H_\theta}{\partial\phi}\right] = 4\pi j_r + \frac{1}{c}\frac{\partial D_r}{\partial t},$$

$$\frac{1}{r}\left[\frac{1}{\sin\theta}\frac{\partial H_r}{\partial\phi} - \frac{\partial}{\partial r}(rH_\phi)\right] = 4\pi j_\theta + \frac{1}{c}\frac{\partial D_\theta}{\partial t},$$

$$\frac{1}{r}\left[\frac{\partial}{\partial r}(rH_\theta) - \frac{\partial H_r}{\partial\theta}\right] = 4\pi j_\phi + \frac{1}{c}\frac{\partial D_\phi}{\partial t};$$

and there was light.

'I am developing the opinion that the only way of explaining the creation is to show that the creator had absolutely no job at all to do, and so might as well not have existed. We can track down the infinitely lazy creator, the creator totally free of any labour of creation, by resolving apparent complexities into simplicities, and I hope to find a way of expressing, at the end of the journey, how a non-existent creator can be allowed to evaporate into nothing and to disappear from the scene.'
PROFESSOR PETER ATKINS

But the fears of certain theologians and the hopes of some non-theists rest on insecure foundations. Atkins' 'infinitely lazy creator' is simply Coulson's 'God-of-the-gaps' by another name.

'God-of-the-Gaps'

EXAMPLE	'GOD-OF-THE-GAPS' TALK
Scientists have found that matter is made up of atoms (19th Century)	'But they won't be able to split the atom. You can't unmake what God has made.'
Scientists trace the origins of the universe to a Big Bang (20th Century)	'But they won't understand how the Big Bang itself started. God did that'.
Cosmologists know that stars were made by hydrogen collecting under gravity (20th Century)	'Alright, but they'll never unravel the mystery of "black holes". That's God's secret.'
The human genome sequence has been completed (21st Century)	'Maybe, but they will never be able to make things live. Only God can do that!'

Reductionism

Going down ...

There is a hierarchy of scientific explanations, given at different levels. **Social science** explains our behaviour in society; **psychology** explains individual behaviour, including how belief-changes take place; **biology** explains our bodies at the level of cells; chemistry explains the large organic molecules comprising them; and **physics** explains the atoms making them up – the protons, neutrons and electrons making up the atoms; and the quarks composing them... like unpeeling an onion! Does it ever stop?

The reduction of higher levels to lower ones is a powerful method of science called **methodological reductionism**. For example, using the billiard-ball model, it is possible to treat gas pressure as resulting from myriads of bombardments of tiny elastic particles in constant, rapid motion. This enables the relationship between gas-pressure and volume (Boyle's Law) to be derived without needing to enter a laboratory. Methodological reductionism and statements such as 'we are made of atoms and molecules' offer no threat to religious belief.

But some people smuggle in a couple of extra words, claiming 'we are *nothing but* atoms and molecules'. They

'Many scientific advances have been interpreted, either triumphantly or with apprehension, as blows against religion. To some extent, this situation is more the fault of theologians than of scientists; the theological position of the "god-of-the-gaps" has probably done more damage to theology than anything else.'

Dr J.S.R. Goodlad in Science for Non-scientists

assert that matter/energy is all there is — a position called **naturalism**. Since philosophical theories about 'what there is' go under the heading of ontology, this belief is called **ontological reductionism**. The give-away words of this debunking tactic are 'nothing but' (and similar words like 'only' and 'just'), so it has been dubbed 'nothing-buttery'.

'Nothing-buttery'

If a boy said to his girlfriend, 'I love you, even though you're nothing but...

- enough phosphorus to make 2,000 matches

- enough iron to make a medium sized nail

- enough chlorine to disinfect a swimming pool

- enough fat for ten bars of soap'

...he would soon be looking for a new girlfriend! Certainly we *are* made up of chemicals such as carbon, oxygen, nitrogen, sulphur and phosphorus, which would only cost a few pounds or dollars if purchased separately. But we are far from being *nothing but* chemicals. The book of Genesis says that we are made of 'dust', but also that we are made 'in the image of God'.

'Nothing but' makes a difference

1. 'Sentences are collections of letters of the alphabet'
2. 'Sentences are nothing but collections of letters of the alphabet'
aabde ee e hhiiiknnn oooop rsssst uuy

Clearly there is a difference between this and the same collection set out as below:
there is a poisonous snake behind you

It is only true that 'sentences are nothing but collections of letters of the alphabet' in the trivial sense that if all the letters are removed, nothing would be left. But it would be misleading to imply the list says everything, even in the right order. A new property has emerged – the *meaning*. There is a threat, requiring instant action.

Going up... emergence

It is economical to express everything in the universe in terms of about 100 basic building-bricks, or elements, each made up of a smaller range of 'elementary particles'. But methodological reductionism can result in overlooking **arrangement**, giving properties that individual 'building-bricks' do not have. If hydrogen and oxygen are mixed together, we are left with gases. But if they combine together, they form a more complex substance – water. An **emergent property**, 'wetness', arises from large collections of water molecules.

All atoms of carbon are alike, but if joined differently, either graphite or diamond may result. Carbon is special in forming an enormous number of compounds, so complicated that a new property may emerge – the ability to replicate – thus crossing the border between living and non-living things. Consciousness (awareness of the external world) arises only above certain levels of complexity and is another example of emergence.

The emergence of meaning identifies a critic of C.S. Lewis' idea of 'transposition' (p. 29) as an 'ontological reductionist'. As Lewis puts it:

'The strength of such a critic lies in the words "merely" or "nothing but". He sees all the facts but not the meaning. Quite truly, therefore, he claims to have seen all the facts. There is nothing else there except the meaning. He is therefore, as regards the matter in hand, in the position of an animal. You will have noticed that most dogs cannot understand pointing. You point to a bit of food on the floor: the dog, instead of looking at the floor, sniffs at your finger. A finger is a finger to him, and that is all. His world is all fact and no meaning.'

Nothing-buttery...

'...has been the major contributory factor to the widespread acceptance in society that science and religious belief are not only in conflict, but that science has made religion completely superfluous.'

Levels of explanation

Here is a reductionist account of two (actual) books – a paperback copy of the Bible and a copy of last year's railway timetable.

• At the atomic level both consist of a similar collection of the 92 naturally occurring elements. They might therefore be seen as essentially the same.

• At the next level up both consist chemically of carbon, in the form of printer's ink on cellulose, and they may have similar masses, volumes and shapes; so again, they are practically the same.

• Even at the next level up their compositions show little difference. Each has sheets of paper joined at one edge, with stiff material outside. The black printer's ink is shaped in a similar number of distinct forms. At this level, the two books are still virtually the same, even though the timetable has more numbers than letters. Many of these groups of letters are the same – the words.

But what is distinctive is the **syntax**, the way the words are organized into sentences, to give them meaning. On this basis, one book is out of date and practically useless, while the other is in many respects timeless. Organizing words into sentences results in the emergence of new properties such as meaning and purpose. In one case it means trains could have been expected at particular times with the purpose of enabling customers to plan journeys. In the other, 'the primary purpose of the sacred writings,' said Galileo, is 'the service of God and the salvation of souls'.

'...one of the major objections presented is that science... offers a complete and satisfying explanation of how we got here and what we are.'

DR RODNEY HOLDER

Explaining Away?

It is easy to imagine scientific explanations 'explaining away' any purpose for which we and the universe are here. Hence some religious people find explanations of religious experience threatening and debunking. But religious experience is part of human behaviour and is open to scientific explanation by psychologists and sociologists. So how might psychologists, acting in their professional capacity, explain religious experience? It should not, of course, be assumed that psychologists are irreligious; some are, others are not. They might, though less frequently today, talk about a **stimulus** arousing us, our **response** being the actions we take, and the **reinforcement** being whatever encourages us to continue with our beliefs. Christian accounts could equally refer to God's action in people's lives, using words such as 'repentance' (change of mind), 'conversion' (change of direction), and 'regeneration' (new birth) through the work of God's Spirit.

The issue of truth

A key question is whether the religious beliefs are true or not. Obviously if drugs are used as a stimulus to change people's beliefs, psychiatric explanations might be able to explain away either the appearance or the disappearance of those beliefs. Where beliefs are true, however, various types of explanations can be valid, compatible and complete in their own terms:

'Explaining' is not 'explaining away'
'Naming' is not 'explaining'

Labelling a religious experience as 'psychological' *explains* nothing. It simply says what we already know, that it is one aspect of human behaviour; but so too is doubt.

Sociologists are particularly interested in **functionalism**, the role religion plays in a social group (perhaps to legitimate authority), and what encourages the growth or decline of religious beliefs within a society. Psychology and sociology are concerned with the **causes** of belief rather than the **grounds** for judging them true or false. There is nothing wrong with methodologically 'bracketing out' truth, so long as it is remembered that:

• These are partial ways of looking at human behaviour.

• They are not substitutes for the importance of examining the truth or falsehood of the beliefs themselves.

4. Belief, Faith and Evidence

Everyone has beliefs, such as:

- There is life on other planets.

- Performing a particular dance makes it rain.

- Repeating scientific experiments gives identical results.

- There is no God.

- The last train has gone.

- The world is real and not a dream.

Beliefs may be true or false. How do we test them?

Finding Truth

A belief may be said to be true if, and only if, it corresponds with things as they actually are. Pointers to truth include:

- Comprehensiveness: taking into account all known, relevant data.

- Consistency: free from internal contradictions.

- Coherence: holding together, making overall sense.

Postmodernism is associated with relativism, the denial that any one set of beliefs is more true than another. 'Truth' sometimes degenerates from correspondence with what is the case, to little more than 'what individuals feel comfortable with'. Phrases such as 'true for you' imply it may not be 'true' for someone else. But truth can be uncomfortable; and truth-telling costly to practise.

Beliefs are powerfully affected by culture. Someone born in

'Truth is in the mind of the thinker, according to the subjectivist, or arises from the collective agreement of a society, according to the relativist. The objectivist, on the other hand, holds that truth is a goal which we aim at but do not necessarily reach.'

Professor Roger Trigg

an Islamic country may grow up a Muslim. Somebody whose parents are atheists may adopt their views. But the key issue is not majority opinion or pressure to conform, but whether there are adequate *grounds* for claiming the belief is true.

Relativism, by denying absolute truth, encounters the problem of **reflexivity**; it trips itself up. If there are no absolute truths about beliefs, what about the central belief of relativism: that 'there are no absolute truths and all is relative'? True or false? If true, relativism is false, because at least one thing – its central belief – is true! If the belief is false, it can be discounted. Furthermore, if all beliefs are relative to particular societies, so too is the relativist's central belief, thereby forfeiting any claim to being universally true. The position is **self-referentially incoherent**. It saws off the branch it is sitting on and illustrates the tendency to see our own pronouncements as exempt from the tests we apply to others.

Party-talk

A church-goer, when introduced to a physicist at a party, regarded him as 'on the other side'. He believed there were absolutes in life, but thought Einstein had said everything was relative. The physicist also happened to be a church-goer and quickly pointed out that the only similarity between **relativism** and Einstein's theories of **relativity** was the words. Einstein's theories actually embody a great 'absolute' – the velocity of light *in vacuo*.

Content, causes and grounds for belief

Questions	To obtain answers	Focus
What beliefs do people hold?	Researchers conduct surveys and study world religions	Content of belief
What causes people to hold religious beliefs?	Psychologists, sociologists and anthropologists investigate factors that encourage or discourage holding religious beliefs	Causes of belief
Are the beliefs true?	Philosophers, theologians and historians examine claims that God exists and has spoken to us	Grounds for belief

Causes of belief

These may include subjective factors such as need of security, fear, or family influence. There is nothing wrong with these, even fear, if something needs avoiding for our good. Family upbringing, however, does not guarantee the truth of beliefs, so two extremes need avoiding:

A matter of upbringing?

A student once said to Archbishop William Temple, 'You believe what you believe because of the way you were brought up.' To which Temple replied, 'That is as it may be. But the fact remains that you believe that I believe what I believe because of the way I was brought up, because of the way you were brought up.'

• Adopting these beliefs without thinking them through.

• Rejecting them simply to be different!

Neither are adequate foundations for a set of beliefs to live by.

The influence of upbringing has led to a misconception, called the 'genetic fallacy' (from *genesis* meaning 'origins'), that beliefs can be explained away by recounting how they arise. If that were so, it would also damage the sceptical position since, as with relativism, self-reference comes in.

Volition

Our wills are involved in believing, in addition to our understanding.

'If someone very much wants not to believe, all the evidence in the world will probably not convince him. If he wants to believe he may be far too uncritical in his original assessment and then run into difficulties afterwards.'
DR OLIVER BARCLAY

Since actions result from beliefs, our wills in turn affect our choices of action.

If only the will were involved in believing, we might call the belief 'credulity'.

'I can't believe that!' said Alice.

'Can't you?' the Queen said in a pitying tone. 'Try again: draw a long breath, and shut your eyes.'

Alice laughed. 'There's no use trying,' she said: 'one can't believe impossible things.'

'I dare say you haven't had much practice,' said the Queen. 'When I was your age, I always did it for half an hour a day. Why, sometimes I've believed as many as six impossible things before breakfast.'

LEWIS CARROLL

Grounds for belief

These are objective factors that are independent of whether anyone believes them or not.

'An ungrounded belief is easily swayed and abandoned, even though it might be correct.'

PROFESSOR DAVID WOLFE

The following beliefs illustrate the distinction between **causes** and **grounds**. For each there is a cause, signalled by 'because'. But there are not grounds for each.

• Sarah believed she had won the prize because her 'lucky number' was on her ticket.

• Sarah believed she had won the prize because Chris said she had seen her name on the list of prize winners.

• Sarah believed she had won the prize because she had seen her name and number on the official list of prize winners.

Unknown to Sarah, Chris was lying. It was still true that Sarah's name was on the list and that she had won. So Sarah believed the right thing for the wrong reason. But she was not justified in believing it, even though it was true. Only in the last instance would there have been adequate grounds for believing she had won. In that case we would say, 'Sarah *knew* she had won the draw', rather than 'Sarah *believed* she had won it.'

'There are only two kinds of people in the end: those who say to God, "Thy will be done," and those to whom God says, in the end, "Thy will be done."'

Professor C.S. Lewis

Although we can believe things that may be true or false, we can only know things that are true. Normally we say we know something if we are sure about it. If we find we were wrong, we can still say 'I believed it, but I was wrong'; but not, 'I knew it, but I was wrong.'

Some philosophers define knowledge as 'justified, true belief'. Beliefs lie somewhere on a line between knowledge and opinion. Justification depends on evidence, which leads us to the next point.

Evidence

Evidence may be direct or indirect; and it may be cumulative.

You could be justified in believing you had missed your last train from the direct evidence of your senses; you saw it go. If someone asks, 'Are you sure that was the last train?' you might appeal to indirect evidence: 'The station clock shows it's well past its departure time; this is its usual platform and the signal's at red.' But platform alterations

can occur and trains sometimes make late starts. If the porter said it was your train, however, you might decide the cumulative evidence of these many valid small clues added up to a convincing whole – 'I know I've missed it!' – and face a taxi-fare or a long walk home.

'Ten-leaky-buckets-Tactic'

It is important to distinguish between a genuine cumulative case and a spurious one. As Professor Anthony Flew cautions:

> '*Nor, incidentally, will it do to recognize that of a whole series of arguments each individually is defective, but then to urge that nevertheless in sum they comprise an impressive case... We have here to insist upon a sometimes tricky distinction: between, on the one hand, the valid principle of the accumulation of evidence, where every item has at least some weight in its own right; and, on the other hand, the Ten-leaky-buckets-Tactic, applied to arguments none of which hold water at all.*'

In detective work, direct evidence may come from witnesses, but much evidence is likely to be indirect. Cumulative cases may be built up from many fragments of valid evidence. If 'little grey cells' solve the case, one explanation will be found to be true, while the others are shown to be false.

Proof

If the accused is to be found guilty in a court of law, proof beyond reasonable doubt will be required. In legal language: 'proof of such a convincing character that you would be willing to rely and act upon it without hesitation in the most important of your own affairs. However, it does not mean an absolute certainty.'

This forensic definition also serves our present purposes because the word 'proof' has come, in many people's eyes, to mean 'showing beyond all possible doubt'; which is virtually impossible except in logic and some branches of mathematics. What *is* realistic is to require evidence sufficient for action. Actions are tied inextricably to beliefs, as the following philosophers emphasize:

'... preparedness to act upon what we affirm is admitted on all hands to be the sole, the genuine, the unmistakeable criterion of belief '.

PROFESSOR ALEXANDER BAIN

'... belief has no meaning, except in reference to our actions'.

PROFESSOR R.B. BRAITHWAITE

The archaic meaning of 'proof' as testing is more realistic. The knight-in-shining-armour 'proved' his sword if it did not break in combat. The Woomera Rocket Range in Australia was once called a rocket-*proving* ground. The phrase 'the exception *proves* the rule' similarly uses 'proves' in the sense of testing, though it is often quoted erroneously by someone who loses an argument, but imagines they won!

Scientific laws cannot be 'proved' to hold in every untried experiment. In general, one cannot argue from particular instances like 'these swans are white', to universal conclusions, such as 'all swans are white'. One Australian black swan will falsify it. This is the **problem of induction**.

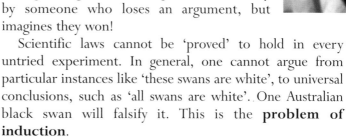

Because science cannot prove (or verify) things beyond question, some philosophers see the task of science as trying to **disprove** (or **falsify**). A hypothesis is made, followed by attempts to knock it down. Lack of success entitles using it for the present. It is unusual, however, for a theory to be overthrown by one experiment. Mistakes may have been made or the results misinterpreted. The rejection of a theory usually awaits a better replacement.

Professor Thomas Kuhn described how science proceeds from a pre-scientific stage to a settled period of 'normal science', interrupted by crises leading to 'extraordinary science' and 'scientific revolutions', from which new theories emerge. An example is Einstein's ideas of space–time modifying Newton's views of space, time and mass.

The general tests for truth, comprehensiveness, consistency and coherence (p. 40), can be applied in science. Here are two more:

- Compactness/economy of explanations/simplicity

'... it is vain to do with more what can be done with fewer'. This principle, formulated over 700 years ago, is known as Ockham's Razor because it cuts off what is superfluous. Following rigorous tests of one simple scientific law (Ohm's Law), James Clerk Maxwell commented, 'the simplicity of an empirical law may be an argument for its exactness'.

- Charm/elegance
Equations and theories that are considered 'elegant' or 'beautiful' in mathematics and science, are thought more likely to be true. In physics, Einstein's famous equation $E = mc^2$ is a good example of both these tests. In mathematics it is claimed 'Beauty is the first test; there is no permanent place in the world for ugly mathematics.'

In everything we have to be satisfied with grounds that are sufficient for the belief to be *warranted*, but which fall short of absolute certainty. The demand 'prove to me God exists' is unrealistic if it means 'demonstrate in a way nobody could question'. In religion, evidence for God is not the same as evidence for electrons, although the evidence is indirect in both cases. The general tests for truth, listed above, also apply to religious beliefs. Something that starts tentatively may end in strong conviction, resulting from cumulative cases, in both science and in religion, as illustrated by the physicist, Professor Sir Robert Boyd:

> *'When I first started doing research in physics the theory of the force between particles in the atomic nucleus was high on the list of important topics, and I recall how each new discovery gave rise to a different theory; or to look at it in another way, the number of possible modifications in the theory was roughly equal to the number of known facts. That situation is one with which the scientist is familiar, and it is a warning that something is wrong, that understanding has not yet been reached. It is required of true understanding that it brings coherence, makes sense of the whole. As I consider the things about Jesus of Nazareth, for me, at any rate, there seems to be only one possible conclusion. It is the one to which Saul the persecutor came in a flash upon the Damascus road: "God was in Christ reconciling the world to himself."'*

IN SCIENCE, INDIRECT EVIDENCE...

... from earthquakes helps geologists build a cumulative case for Earth's liquid core and an inner solid core.

... for a charged atomic particle may come from a vapour trail in a cloud chamber; rather like that produced by a high-flying aircraft.

IN RELIGION, INDIRECT EVIDENCE...

... for God's existence has been inferred from:

• The existence of the universe. The concept of God is of a non-material, uncreated being who, among other things, created everything there is, except himself.

A bus hanging from a damaged highway after the Kobe earthquake in 1995, Hyogo Japan.

To ask 'Who made God?', as though 'God' was some material thing, among other material things, suffers from the weakness of arguments from analogy. It is meaningless and entangles itself in an infinite regress of 'Who created God?' If 'God' had been created, he would not have been 'God'; whatever created him would have been 'God'.

- The nature of the universe (pp. 67–69).

- The existence of moral order.

- Claims of 'divine revelation' (being told things that one could not otherwise know) through prophets and inspired writings. Although science cannot tell us whether there is a God or not, science may help to establish factual details which have a bearing on religious records, for example, the appearance of the Star of Bethlehem,[2] the date of the Crucifixion,[3] and archaeology. If so, it increases confidence in the reliability of religious claims in those records that are not amenable to scientific tests.

- (In Christianity) the incarnation and resurrection of Christ.

- The evidential value of religious experience.

- The 'Five Ways' put forward by Thomas Aquinas (c.1225–74) are examined in books on the philosophy of religion, and may be seen as possible pointers rather than proofs.

It would be misleading to imagine that everyone viewing the same evidence reaches the same conclusion. 'Seeing' is 'seeing-as'. Perceptions, interpretations, previous experience and willingness to entertain ideas vary. Most people are familiar with illusions such as the old lady/young woman.

Dismissive comments such as 'it's all a matter of interpretation' might suggest that religious belief is just a matter of personal preference. But not all interpretations are equally valid; some fit the data better than others, whether we like it or not. Sometimes searching is prized more highly than finding: seeking can be challenging; finding could involve a change in lifestyle.

'There comes a moment when the children who have been playing at burglars hush suddenly: was that a real footstep in the hall? There comes a moment when people who have been dabbling in religion ('Man's search for God'!) suddenly draw back. Supposing we really found him? We never meant it to come to that! Worse still, supposing he had found us?'
PROFESSOR C.S. LEWIS

Doubt

'... tell me what you believe in. I have plenty of doubts of my own.'
GOETHE

'It is a world in which doubt is not only a permissible thing, but in which doubt is the indispensable method of aiming at truth.'
PROFESSOR C.A. COULSON

Doubts come unbidden both to believers and non-believers in God. Professor Sir Fred Hoyle, well-known for his anti-religious views, was disturbed by a 'multiple coincidence' leading to the existence of carbon in quantity, necessary for life as we know it:

'Would you not say to yourself... "Some supercalculating intellect must have designed the properties of the carbon atom, otherwise the chance of my finding such an atom through the blind forces of nature would be utterly minuscule"? Of course you would... You would conclude that the carbon atom is a fix... and that there are no blind forces worth speaking about in nature.'

Critical thinking is important. In *academia* the more you study, the more questions you find, which helps stimulate

> '... the fact that some understanding is required for intelligent faith does not mean that complete understanding is necessary. Without some knowledge, faith would be superstition. With full knowledge there would be no need for faith at all. Faith is reason exploring, it is reason become courageous, it goes beyond the evidence but it is not actually denied by the evidence.'
>
> *Professor John Hull*

interest. There are also answers! Doubts can be seen positively, as places of intellectual and spiritual growth. The 'yo-yo' mentality, whereby every unanswered question throws *everything* in doubt, has inadequacies. Unanswered questions are best placed in a 'suspense account', awaiting further understanding. After all, we know very little of what there is to know.

Faith

'If I have faith, it means that I have decided to do something and am willing to stake my life on it. When Columbus started on his first voyage into the West, he believed that the earth was round and small enough to be circumnavigated. He did not think that this was right in theory alone, but he staked his whole existence on it.'

PROFESSOR WERNER HEISENBERG, BEST-KNOWN FOR HIS PRINCIPLE OF INDETERMINACY

Faith involves launching out into the unknown on the strength of the known. Other sea-captains had access to the same slim evidence that was available to Columbus; but they did not set sail and so never discovered a New World.

Faith is sometimes mischievously misunderstood as wishful thinking, a blind leap in the dark or believing what you know isn't true! It has been whimsically charicatured as 'an illogical belief in the occurrence of the improbable' and caricatured in two common dichotomies; 'faith-versus-reason' and 'facts-versus-faith' – hence the takeoff: 'Don't confuse me with facts, my faith is made up'! Contrasting facts and faith is fraught with difficulties.

So-called 'facts' involve elements of belief, while beliefs are not simply matters of personal preference, but involve external evidence. The Bible contrasts *faith* with *sight*, not *reason*, which it encourages. It is all too easy to set up such

'straw men' and then to pour scorn on faith, while remaining oblivious of how few thinking believers would recognize any of these positions as theirs.

Another naïve claim about faith is that 'it doesn't matter what you believe as long as you are sincere'. Sincerity is a good thing, but it is possible to be sincerely wrong, as in tragic accidents when patients are given wrong medicines.

Faith is always *in* something; it cannot stand alone. It is the *objects of faith* that matter and these vary enormously in their trustworthiness. For example, people put their faith in friends, medicines, lucky numbers, surgeons, football pool systems, God, newspaper reports, ladders, internet articles, horoscopes, banks, secondhand-car salesmen and husbands/wives.

But imagine a newly-wed, constantly wanting assurance of his wife's fidelity, hiring a private detective to monitor her

Departure of Christopher Columbus from Palos. Spanish School, nineteenth century.

53

Common sense

Common sense is 'what everybody knows'. Using common sense can help avoid credulity, but can mislead by judging what is rational from what is already known. Something novel, that appears incredible, may get rejected, even if true. Common sense is important, but alone it is inadequate as a reliable guide to the unknown.

• At the start of the twentieth century, it ran contrary to common sense to think so-called 'solid matter' is mainly space, but now we accept it.

• Einstein's theories of relativity well-illustrate the limitations of common sense. When they first appeared, a wise editor of *Scientific American* wrote: 'We are tempted to laugh at him, to tell him that the phenomena he suggests are absurd because they contradict these concepts [time, space and mass]. Nothing could be more rash... We must be quite as well prepared to have these conditions reveal some epoch-making fact as was Galileo...'

• More recently, common sense would have ridiculed the idea of cutting up a transparent photograph, shining a light through one of the pieces and seeing the whole picture. But with the development of lasers and holograms it can be done, with a loss of some picture detail.

It is easy to dismiss religious claims, such as incarnation and resurrection, that appear to contradict common sense; but if God is at work, our expectations may need widening to encompass the unfamiliar.

movements. What a basis for marriage! Faith involves trust, suspending disbelief when there are reasonable grounds for doing so. 'Credulity' is the correct word for being too ready to believe when there is insufficient weight of evidence, or even contrary evidence.

Faith, in its religious sense, is comparable to trust in a person. It includes faith *that* something is true, but it goes beyond faith that God exists or that he created the world. Faith in God means trust in, confidence in, and reliance on God. It includes dependence on God for forgiveness and help in living; it involves commitment — but not to fence-sitting.

Religious faith must be well-grounded in facts to be rationally believed. The most persuasive evidence for the believer is likely to be the experience of a personal encounter with God, but this belongs in the *private domain* and may not convince another person who has not had such an experience. The onlooker may, however, be influenced by what is in the *public domain*, such as a visible and compatible lifestyle, as the apostle James insists:

> '*Show me your faith without deeds, and I will show you my faith by what I do. You believe that there is one God. Good! Even the demons believe that – and shudder.*'
>
> JAMES 2:18–19

But in the end, the Christian faith, for example, claims to be based on evidence in the public domain, such as that already listed, including the evidence of history. Did Jesus live? What did he teach? Did he rise from the dead? These matters will be explored in the next chapter.

5. *Miracles*

'It was a miracle she climbed out of the wreckage alive.'
'Passing that exam was nothing short of a miracle.'
'He was healed when they prayed for him; it's a miracle!'

What is a Miracle?

The word 'miracle' is popularly used to express amazement, but in its usual religious sense it means:

* Something amazing, a **spectacle**, which attracts attention by its nature, timing, or both.

* An event that is **significant**, intended by God as a sign.

In Jewish history, Moses showed Pharaoh various miracles as signs that God demanded the Israelites' release from Egyptian slavery. Pharaoh's magicians are recorded as duplicating some of them; so not all miracles are claimed as due to God's power. Physical explanations are not usually given, since trying to guess the 'how?' may distract from the 'why?' Nevertheless, the writer of the book of Exodus says the Red Sea/Sea of Reeds became passable because 'all that night the Lord drove the sea back with a strong east wind' (Exodus 14:21).[4]

Miracle stories were common in New Testament times, but are also found earlier and later; and in other world religions. Two main groups involve nature miracles like the 'stilling of the storm' (Luke 8:22–25) and healing miracles like that of Jairus' daughter (Mark 5:22–43). Three main words for miracle occur in the New Testament, and Acts 2:22 uses them all: 'Jesus of Nazareth was a man accredited by God to you by miracles [*dunamis*, an 'act of authority, of power'], wonders [*teras*] and signs [*semeion*], which God did among you through him…'

God at Work in the World

It would be arrogant to think that people in earlier times were stupid by comparison with us. They knew that it was not 'natural' for virgins to have sons, or for people to rise from the dead. The meaning of 'natural' here is what normally occurs.

The opposite to this sense of natural appears to be 'supernatural'; but this can perpetuate a common belief that only supernatural events are God's activity, encapsulated in phrases such as, 'It's not God, it's just natural.' This belief limited the usefulness of the cosmic clockmaker model that could be interpreted as God making the clock, winding it and leaving it to run, which virtually amounted to atheism. The deists considered it beneath God's dignity to interfere with the orderly 'clockwork' of the universe if he had made it properly in the first place. Some semi-deists believed God might 'intervene' to perform the occasional miracle, much as a clockmaker might wind the clock or poke tweezers in to adjust the mechanism. But miracles are not God acting where he does not normally act, but acting differently from normal. Events are only miracles within an orderly

framework, since they are only extraordinary through knowing what is ordinary. Perhaps normal/unusual, or ordinary/extraordinary acts of God is clearer than the ambiguous words 'natural' and 'supernatural'.

The New Testament presents Jesus Christ as the agent, both of creating and sustaining the world.

> *'(Christ) is the image of the invisible God... by him all things were created... in him all things hold together.'*
> COLOSSIANS 1:15–17

> *'...in these last days God has spoken to us by his Son... through whom he made the universe. The Son is the radiance of God's glory and the exact representation of his being, sustaining all things by his powerful word.'*
> HEBREWS 1:2–3

The idea of a creation that is dynamic rather than static needs a different model from a clock. Professor Donald MacKay, a researcher in the mechanisms of the brain, suggested a television picture:

> *'Imagine... an artist able to bring his world into being, not by laying down paint on canvas, but by producing an extremely rapid succession of sparks of light on the screen of a television tube... The world he invents is now not static but dynamic, able to change and evolve at his will. Both its form and its law of change (if any) depend on the way in which he orders the sparks of light in space and time. The scene is steady and unchanging just for as long as he wills it so; but if he were to cease his activity, his invented world would not become chaotic; it would simply cease to be.'*

Miracles and Scientific 'Laws'

The claim, 'Science says miracles are impossible because they would "break" scientific laws' expresses one perceived difficulty about miracles. The word 'law' may originally have been used in science because the orderliness of nature reflects the order laws bring to society. It has proved confusing to use the same word for both.

- Laws of the land are **prescriptive**: they say what *should* be done and prescribe what *ought* to be, as an architect's plans prescribe what should be built, or a doctor's prescription states what medicine should be supplied.

- Scientific laws are **descriptive**: they say what *does* (normally) happen, describing what *is*, as a map describes the lie of the land.

Scientific laws cannot be 'obeyed' or 'broken' and they no more 'govern' events than a map 'governs' the coastline. This is all loose talk drawn from the other kind of law. Events may be 'in accordance/not in accordance' with scientific laws.

The descriptive/prescriptive distinction should not be pressed too far. Scientific laws do prescribe something – our expectations about what is normal, based on precedent. But they provide no guarantees against things being otherwise.

There is nothing unalterable about scientific laws. For instance, Boyle's Law, mentioned earlier (p. 35), says 'the volume of a fixed mass of gas at constant temperature varies inversely with the pressure'. At high pressures Boyle's Law does not hold and a more complicated law is needed.

Robert Boyle (1627–91), Irish born chemist and physicist, painted around 1690 by Johann Kerseboom.

Two Remarkable Claims

We now turn to consider two of the most 'eyebrow-raising' claims made by any religion:

1. Incarnation – God entering our world.

2. Resurrection – Jesus Christ rising from the dead.

Incarnation

The brief story in the box below, using characters created by the children's writer Enid Blyton (with apologies!), is concocted to raise some serious points.

Incongruity is a key feature: the appearance in the story of the author both of Noddy and Bert's 'world' and of their Christmas; her age compared with that of Mr Plod; and author-time being different from actor-time. A few seconds of Enid Blyton's time was sufficient to give Noddy and Bert a two-hour Christmas-shopping trip. The time-scale of the story is the author's creation; it has no being apart from the author. In our world's story, time is part of the created order – a view taken by Augustine and echoed by modern cosmology (p. 65). But whatever could it mean to talk of 'God's time', by analogy with ours?

A Christmas visitor

It was a cold winter's afternoon before Christmas. Noddy and Bert Monkey had just sat down to tea when the doorbell rang. Bert answered it and returned, looking very puzzled. 'Who is it?' said Noddy.

'She says her name's Enid; and wants to come in,' replied Bert Monkey.

'You'd better let her,' said Noddy

A middle-aged lady came in and said 'Hello! My name's Enid Blyton...'

'Never heard of her!' Noddy whispered to Bert. 'Same here,' he replied, 'Christmas is all about cakes and presents – and being left in peace!' he whispered pointedly.

'...but don't bother to tell me your names,' went on the lady, 'I know who you are...'. Noddy and Bert looked baffled.

'I can see you're looking puzzled' said the visitor. 'What I mean is, I know you because I made you – you might even say I created you.'

'What do you mean, you *created* us?' said Noddy crossly. 'You're not even as old as Mr Plod! Don't play jokes; we're tired. We've just spent two hours Christmas shopping!'

'I'm not joking,' said the lady. 'I know it's difficult to understand, but without me you wouldn't have Christmas; and your shopping only took five seconds in my time – but I've got my own shopping to do; I just wanted to drop in to say "Happy Christmas!"'

She left. Bert and Noddy stared, wide-eyed, at each other until Noddy broke the silence with a single word – 'Crackers!' he said.

There have been books and plays in which authors have written themselves into their own stories and even appeared on stage. The writer Dorothy L. Sayers saw God as 'a living author' of a book in which we are all characters. Authors reveal their minds in their books. So Dorothy L. Sayers entitled her book *The Mind of the Maker* and pointed out that, in Christian theology, 'the Mind of the Maker was also incarnate personally and uniquely. Examining our analogy for something to which this may correspond, we may say that God wrote His own autobiography... the author appears, personally and without disguise, as a character in his own story'.

We have already seen the comparison of God to an author in the 'Two Books' metaphor (p. 9). But here the analogy is developed differently, with God as the author of an *autobiography* – a literary device to illustrate the incarnation.

In John's account of the life of Jesus, a passage occurs which has a parallel in the Noddy story: 'Your father Abraham rejoiced at the thought of seeing my day; he saw it and was glad', said Jesus. His puzzled hearers replied, 'you are not yet fifty years old... and you have seen Abraham!' (John 8:56–57).

'Autobiography', continues Dorothy Sayers, 'is an infallible self-betrayal. The truth about the writer's personality will out, in spite of itself... If, however, the author either consciously or unconsciously tries to incarnate himself as something other than what he is, there will be a falseness in the artistic expression... the truth of what he says about himself is tested by the truth of the form in which he says it... For this reason, no considerations of false reverence should prevent us from subjecting the incarnations of creators to the severest tests of examination... the writing of autobiography is a dangerous business; it is a mark of either great insensitiveness to danger or of an almost supernatural courage. Nobody but a god can pass unscathed through the searching ordeal of incarnation.'

Resurrection

The Romans crucified multitudes; Josephus records 2,000 on a single occasion. One crucifixion is remembered the world over, singled out by the almost incredible claim that Jesus of Nazareth had risen physically from death to the power of an endless life! John records Jesus foretelling this: 'I lay down my life... I have authority to lay it down and authority to take it up again' (John 10:17–18). How does one conceive of such a happening? Is it comparable to the 're-embodiment' of computer software in new hardware after the original machine has been wrecked by vandals?

Common sense does not help with unprecedented events. Only evidence can adjudicate. Everyone who is reported as having seen Jesus after the crucifixion has died, so no direct evidence is available; only indirect historical evidence that might build up to a cumulative case. On the positive side, the written evidence for the events surrounding the life of Jesus far exceeds that for anyone else of comparable antiquity, some coming from non-biblical sources, such as Josephus, Tacitus and Pliny.

Those who disbelieve the resurrection dismiss the accounts as embellished stories, legends or deliberate inventions. They claim that the body was stolen by the disciples, the authorities or grave robbers; or that the disciples mistook the tomb in the early morning light; or that Jesus did not die and the resurrection appearances were hallucinations. But there are difficulties with each of these claims. For example:

- The historian, Tacitus (c. 56–120 CE), records that the crucifixion of Jesus 'checked that pernicious superstition for a short time, but it broke out afresh'.

- The carefully guarded Jewish Sabbath became, for many, the Christian 'Sunday'.

- A group of disillusioned men, ashamed of their cowardly behaviour at the arrest of their leader, suddenly became bold. In the words of the New Testament, they then 'turned the world upside down' and were prepared to suffer and die for it.

Professor Norman Anderson, a lawyer, listed evidence that might be submitted in a court of law.[5]

Another lawyer, writing under the name of Frank Morrison, set out to write a book 'to sift some of the evidence at first hand' for his earlier belief that Jesus' 'history rested upon very insecure foundations'. His book, *Who Moved the Stone?*, written rather like a detective story, describes how his research led to the opposite conviction,

the historicity of the resurrection, and how he came to write a very different book.

It matters whether the resurrection happened. Paul writes, '...if Christ has not been raised, our preaching is useless and so is your faith' (1 Corinthians 15:14). It is not an optional extra but something by which Christianity stands or falls – the **falsification criterion** Professor Flew was demanding in the 1950s. Since power over death was seen as belonging to God, if the claim were true, the implications would be far-reaching. Other clues might be gleaned from Jesus' use of titles such as 'Lord' and 'Son of God', as well as the personal name 'I am', which God had spoken to Moses. More than this, as C.S. Lewis highlights, Jesus made the ultimate claim:

'...the claim to forgive sins: any sins. Now unless the speaker is God, this is really so preposterous as to be comic. We can all understand how a man forgives offences against himself. You tread on my toe and I forgive you, you steal my money and I forgive you. But what should we make of a man, himself unrobbed and untrodden on, who announced that he forgave you for treading on other men's toes and stealing other men's money? Asinine fatuity is the kindest description we should give of his conduct. Yet this is what Jesus did. He told people that their sins were forgiven, and never waited to consult all the other people whom their sins had undoubtedly injured. He unhesitatingly behaved as if He was the party chiefly concerned; the person chiefly offended in all offences. This makes sense only if He really was the God whose laws are broken and whose love is wounded in every sin. In the mouth of any speaker who is not God, these words would imply what I can only regard as a silliness and conceit unrivalled by any other character in history.'

6. First and Last Things

In the beginning was a Big Bang, a **singularity** in which the ordinary laws of physics are unlikely to have held. It is all too easy to picture this as a gigantic explosion in empty space at a distant moment in time. But this picture is wrong on two counts: there was no space and no time; they came into being with the Big Bang. So 'In the beginning' is a better phrase than 'Once upon a time'. St Augustine (fourth century CE) said creation was *with* time, not *in* time, since if God was creator of everything, he must have created time. Because we inhabit space–time, its absence is almost inconceivable. But much of modern science is **counterintuitive**, it defies common sense. This is also true at the other end of the scale of size. The fuzzy world of quantum mechanics has shown the inadequacy of the old mechanistic view of a totally predictable universe. What follows is our modern model – our current 'guesstimate' – of the origins of the universe, how it developed and what it is like.

It is important from the start to distinguish between the theological concept of creation and the scientific study of origins. They are not the same thing. 'Creation', theologically, is God's **act** of bringing-and-sustaining-in-being. Science studies the **processes** that resulted in the universe.

Initially, light was everywhere, although 'everywhere' was relatively small; but 'space' grew very rapidly. After about three minutes 98 per cent of the matter that 'condensed out' from the energy (Einstein's $E = mc^2$ links them) consisted of about three-parts hydrogen and one-part helium. The rapid expansion lowered the temperature below what was needed for further elements to arise and the 'nuclear reactor' shut down.

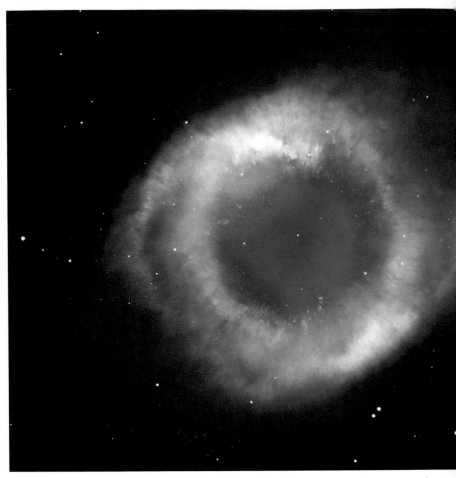

The Helix Nebula, one of the nearest nebulae to Earth, as viewed through the NASA Hubble Space Telescope. Staff at NASA have nicknamed it 'the eye of God'.

Hydrogen and helium were drawn into clumps, under gravity. The bigger they became, the faster more matter was attracted to them and the hotter they became, until the colliding particles started to fuse together into heavier elements. So stars were born. These vast furnaces took over 10 thousand million (billion) years to 'cook up' the hydrogen and helium into heavier elements such as carbon, oxygen, nitrogen – the elements necessary for (carbon-based) life as we know it. Stars are like hydrogen bombs under control and radiation energy is released through fusion. This acts outward, counteracting the inward force of gravity. When the fuel gets used up, gravity wins and, depending on the size of the star, it may implode. This releases enough heat to scatter its outer layers — those newly-formed heavier elements that eventually compose our bodies — in a supernova. As Professor Peter Atkins puts it, 'We are galactic dust, and to galactic dust we shall return.'

So that is a current scientific answer to 'How did the universe develop?' (p. 8). But, 'Was it accidental or planned?' transcends science's ability to address, although it is evasive to dismiss it as a 'non-question'.

Make your choice:

'We are stardust...'

'the ashes of long-dead stars'

'reprocessed nuclear waste'

The Goldilocks Effect

Less than 2 metres tall, with a 'best before' date of some 'three score years and ten', how can we matter in a universe so big and so old; so dark and so cold? Its sheer size and age has been claimed to render us insignificant. But if the universe were not like this, we would not be here. It has taken about 10 billion of the universe's 13.7 billion years for the elements for life to build up in stars. Since space is expanding so fast, its size is enormous, and its rapid expansion cools it down. Many stars cannot be seen because the rapid expansion stops the light reaching us, so it is dark.

Many of the so-called 'constants of nature', like the gravitational constant, appear to be very finely balanced. Minuscule differences would mean our not being here. The universe seems remarkably 'fine-tuned' for life as we know it to be possible:

'The factor by which the universe exceeds us in space and time is not dissimilar to the factor by which we exceed elementary particles. In orders of magnitude we seem to be "midway between the stars and the atoms".'

'... if the relative strengths of the nuclear and electromagnetic forces were to be slightly different then carbon atoms could not exist in Nature and human physicists would not have evolved'.

PROFESSORS JOHN BARROW AND FRANK TIPLER

Had the Big Bang 'explosion differed in strength at the outset by only one part in 10^{60}, the universe we now perceive would not exist'.

PROFESSOR PAUL DAVIES

These cosmic coincidences underpin various expressions of the **Anthropic Cosmological Principle** – dubbed the **Goldilocks Effect** because, like Baby Bear's porridge, chair and bed, things are 'just right'. Even if we were the only carbon-based life there is (and we don't know), the whole universe would be needed for our existence; not just our home galaxy (the Milky Way) of 100 billion stars, but all the other 100 billion galaxies, each containing 100 billion stars, which represent about 20 galaxies for every man, woman and child on Earth!

Does this mean the universe was designed with us in mind? Certainly it is consistent with belief in a purposeful God. But how far does cosmogony get us in a quest for God? Not very far. In 1930 Professor Sir James Jeans wrote: '... from the intrinsic evidence of his creation, the Great Architect of the Universe now begins to appear as a pure mathematician.' But 'architect' and 'mathematician' are remote comparisons for the caring God of the Judeo-Christian tradition.

The Goldilocks Effect is a candidate for some kind of argument for design, but caution is needed. All sorts of other suggestions have been made for these cosmic coincidences. For example, an earlier inflationary stage of the universe might have given rise to them. Nevertheless this just pushes the question back one stage further from 'Why the cosmic coincidences?' to 'Why was the early universe such that it gave rise to the cosmic coincidences that gave rise to us?' An allied speculation is of a **multiverse** – a collection of 'parallel' universes (whatever that might mean) with different physical constants, of which ours just happens to be right for carbon-based life; but even this would not exclude God's activity. Speculations about infinite numbers of universes does, however, raise questions as to whether this offends against Ockham's Razor (p. 47). It is important to distinguish between ideas that are scientific (empirically testable) and those that are currently no more than speculative metaphysics.

'How will it end... "freeze" or "fry"?'

There is a very fine balance between the outward force of the initial Big Bang and the inward attraction of gravity. In 1993, Professor Stephen Hawking wrote:

'If the density of the universe one second after the big bang had been greater by one part in a thousand billion [1,000,000,000,000], the universe would have recollapsed after ten years. On the other hand, if the density of the universe at that time had been less by the same amount, the universe would have been essentially empty since it was about ten years old.'

This would imply a *critical* initial density. Small differences would make our universe uninteresting.

THREE THEORETICAL MODELS:

'Closed universe' Density greater than critical: Gravity wins the tug-of-war, the universe eventually contracts and ends in a 'big crunch'.

'Flat universe' Density equal to critical: Expansion continues for ever, gently enough for interesting developments.

'Open universe' Density less than critical: Expansion is much faster so the universe may become too sparse too quickly for interesting developments.

'Flat' and 'Open' universes end in a 'heat death' as everything approaches the Absolute Zero (-273°C or -460°F). The observed density is only a small fraction of the critical value: 'Open' seems more likely. However, some theoretician's desire for 'Flat' has led to conjectures about an additional, mysterious **dark matter/energy** to get things right.

So, in the closing words of T.S. Eliot's 'The Hollow Men', 'This is the way the world ends / Not with a bang but a whimper.'

But these cosmological models need to be considered alongside theological perspectives on end events (eschatology). Just as the distinction between creation and origins was pointed out earlier, so there is a distinction between a goal for the universe and the last moment of time. In Christian theology the goal is 'to bring all things in heaven and on earth together under one head, even Christ' (Ephesians 1:10). This is realized though Christ's death on the cross, offering forgiveness to all who ask; his promised second coming, the resurrection of the dead and judgment. Finally, in the response of Jesus' disciple Peter, Christians 'wait for what God has promised: new heavens and a new earth, where righteousness will be at home' (2 Peter 3:13).

7. The Galileo Affair

'... the fame of this outstanding genius rests mostly on discoveries he never made, and on feats he never performed. Contrary to statements in even recent outlines of science, Galileo did not invent the telescope; nor the microscope; nor the thermometer; nor the pendulum clock. He did not discover the law of inertia; nor the parallelogram of forces or motions; nor the sun spots. He made no contribution to theoretical astronomy; he did not throw down weights from the leaning tower of Pisa, and did not prove the truth of the Copernican system. He was not tortured by the Inquisition, did not languish in its dungeons, did not say eppur si muove [nevertheless it moves]; and he was not a martyr of science.'

ARTHUR KOESTLER

What Galileo did was to found the modern science of dynamics, which marks his greatness.

In the thirteenth century a detailed attempt had been made by a Catholic theologian and philosopher, Thomas Aquinas, to link Greek science with certain Bible texts. Since the Bible came to be read through Aristotelian spectacles, any attack on Aristotle's physics might seem like an attack on the Bible; so the Galileo affair was:

'Not so much science versus religion as science versus the sanctified science of Aristotle...'
'Superficially it all looks like a paradigm case of what nineteenth-century rationalist historians liked to call the warfare between science and religion... that popular but simplistic formula. The historical reality was much more fascinating and instructive than so crude a polarity would suggest.'

PROFESSOR JOHN BROOKE

It is a story of scientific discovery, personal rivalries and

Ptolemaic geocentric (Earth-centred) system of the Universe, showing the Earth surrounded by water, air and fire representing the four Greek elements and the spheres of the planets and stars. Proposed by Claudius Ptolemy in the second century AD. From Harmonia Macrocosmica by Andreas Cellarius Amsterdam, 1708.

power struggles. Greater diplomacy might have led to a very different outcome. True, there were discussions on biblical interpretation, and struggles over church authority, but not all theologians were against Galileo, nor he against them. The story illustrates how spiritual, moral, social and cultural factors affect science. First, some background is needed about Greek astronomy and Copernicus' ideas.

Circles upon Circles

For 1,500 years the world-view of a Greek astronomer, Ptolemy, held sway. It was this picture that Copernicus challenged.

Ptolemy's views were that:

• The heavens are changeless.

- Heavenly bodies are perfect.
- They move in perfect circles with uniform speed round a central Earth.

The paths of the 'planets' (Greek 'wanderers') caused considerable problems for circular motion, but if planets were imagined to rotate in small circles (epicycles) whose centres moved round large circles, centred on Earth, planetary paths make loops in the heavens. From Earth, the 'loops' are in the plane of the viewer, giving the observed 'forward-stop-backward-stop-forward' motion. By adjusting the speed of rotations and the radii of the epicycles (even adding more), the movement of each planet could be described. Some 80 circles were used, enabling astronomical events such as eclipses to be accurately predicted.

Nicolaus Copernicus

Copernicus (1473–1543) was Polish; he was interested in astronomy and became a canon in Frauenburg Cathedral.

Andreus Nicolaus Copernicus, Polish school, sixteenth century.

> *'The great astronomer saw no conflict between his Christian faith and scientific activity. During his forty years as a canon, Copernicus faithfully served his church with extraordinary commitment and courage. At the same time he studied the world "which has been built for us by the Best and Most Orderly Workman of all".'*
>
> DR CHARLES HUMMEL

Copernicus learned Greek and discovered that not all Greek astronomers held Ptolemy's views. A sun-centred (heliocentric) view was held by Aristarchos in the third century BCE, together with a spinning Earth view. But powerful voices supported a geocentric theory and Aristarchos was accused of sacrilege for challenging the Earth as a divine being and displacing it from a central position. Copernicus, too, believed the Sun was central but was reluctant to publish this, not through fear of religious persecution (as is sometimes maintained), but because he shunned ridicule.

In those days there were better reasons for believing in a moving Sun and a stationary Earth than vice versa:

• The Sun appeared small and looked as if it moved.

• The Earth felt stationary.

• If the Earth went round the Sun in a year, the speed would surely create a wind that would sweep everything off the Earth.

• All bodies were thought to fall to the centre of the universe. Since they fall towards the centre of the Earth, it seemed that the Earth must be central.

Key points about Copernicus' theory

• Copernicus' theory was attractive in suggesting a comprehensive system, instead of Ptolemy's rather untidy scheme that treated every planet separately.

• Contrary to folklore, Copernicus' system did not simplify the complicated system of circles upon circles. It made it somewhat worse. Matters sound simple with a central Sun suggested, but in Copernicus' calculations the planets rotate about the centre of the Earth's orbit, which does not coincide with the centre of the Sun.

• Copernicus was still committed to circular motion. The idea of ellipses came with Kepler's work at the beginning of the seventeenth century. So it required a lot of circles to approximate to elliptical orbits.

• Copernicus' book eventually had far-reaching effects, but created little impact at the time. It was difficult to read and could only be understood by astronomers.

• Copernicus' theory did not arise from measurements alone. These were not particularly accurate. His reasons were partly mystical, citing an ancient Egyptian, Hermes Trismegistus, in support: 'In the midst of all sits Sun enthroned. In this most beautiful temple could we place this luminary in any better position from which he can illuminate the whole at once?... Hermes Trismegistus names him the Visible God.'

- Distant stars did not seem to change position, relative to each other, as they would if the Earth were moving. This effect, called parallax, was too small to be detected at the time.

- A spinning Earth seemed likely to fling off anything that was not fixed.

- An arrow, fired straight up, appeared likely to fall to the west of the firing point because, meanwhile, Earth would continue spinning.

- Birds and clouds, similarly, would drift westwards.

In 1543, the year Copernicus died, his book *De Revolutionibus Orbium Coelestium* (*On the Revolution of the Heavenly Spheres*) was published.

A representation of Copernicus' heliocentric (Sun-centred) scheme showing the Earth circling the Sun which illumines different parts of the globe according to the time of day and the season of the year (1660).

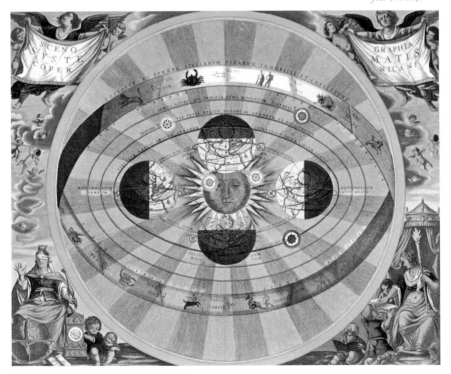

Turning the world upside-down – and putting it straight!

It is often said that Copernicus 'dethroned' humankind by showing Earth was not central. The claim muddles **geocentric** (position) with **anthropocentric** (human importance). It is particularly odd from the pre-Copernican viewpoint of geocentric. According to Aristotle, the world's centre was a sump, a pit into which all debris fell. Of the four supposed 'elements', earth, air, fire and water, earth was densest, so Earth occupied the central position, farthest from the heavens. It is unrealistic to imagine those people thinking themselves important *because* of Earth's centrality, rather the opposite; it was like living at the council tip! Dante, in *The Divine Comedy*, placed hell right at Earth's centre! When Copernicus' work placed Earth among other heavenly bodies, in the region of celestial perfection, far from demoting humans, it elevated their status, giving them citizenship in the heavens!

Copernicus knew full well that a central Sun would mean the universe was vastly bigger than previously imagined, saying: '...as to the place of the earth; although it is not at the centre of the world, nevertheless the distance [to that centre] is as nothing, in particular when compared to that to the fixed stars'. During the seventeenth century it seems that the (approximate) centre of our system, now understood as occupied by the Sun, came to be viewed more positively and this new perception was wrongly imagined as the pre-Copernican view. Yet this legend, like others, is entrenched. Enshrining it in a so-called Copernican principle, namely that 'we do not occupy a privileged position in the Universe', needs a caution attached, according to Professor John Barrow:

'We should be careful not to confuse Copernicus' important lesson that we must not regard our position in the Universe as special in every way with the spurious belief that our position in the Universe cannot therefore be special in any way.'

For instance, relatively small temperature variations ($\pm$ 40 Celsius degrees or $\pm$ 72 Fahrenheit degrees) either side of the ice-point (0 °C or 32°F) need to be maintained for life; and this is very unusual in space.

The English poet, John Milton, who met Galileo shortly before he died, took the trouble to affirm in *Paradise Lost* that Earth's geographical position was irrelevant to its importance; and he showed considerable competence in handling the current technical terms of astronomy.

Farewell to Ptolemy

Greek astronomy was crumbling even before the telescope was invented in 1609. The Sun, viewed through a dark filter, in the 'perfect, unchanging heavens', showed spots that appeared and disappeared. In 1572 a Danish astronomer, Tycho Brahe, saw a new star and later a comet that seemed to cut through the 'crystalline spheres holding the planets'.

Galileo made a telescope and saw bright 'stars' around Jupiter. On different nights he saw two, three and four. Galileo concluded the 'stars' revolved round Jupiter and published his findings in an easy-to-read book, *The Starry Messenger*. He also reported that the Moon had blemishes and the Milky Way was comprised of myriads of stars. Galileo used his growing fame to gain the post of Chief Mathematician and Philosopher at the court of Cosimo II De Medici, Fourth Grand Duke of Tuscany. Galileo wrote saying God had told him to name the four 'stars' of Jupiter the 'Medicean Stars', after the Duke!

Hardly had *The Starry Messenger* been published when Galileo discovered Venus had phases like the Moon. If Copernicus was correct, and Venus circled the Sun, this should happen, but not if Ptolemy was right. Galileo's observations showed that Ptolemy's scheme was wrong, but not that Copernicus was right: Venus' phases also fitted the theory of Tycho Brahe, which had a central Earth, with the Sun and Moon circling it; but that had the other planets simultaneously circling the Sun!

Portrait of Galileo Galilei by Ottavio Mario Leoni, c.1578–1630.

Galileo visited Rome and was given a friendly reception by Pope Paul V. The astronomers of the Jesuit Roman College, initially unconvinced, eventually told their head, Cardinal Bellarmine, that Venus' phases did disprove Ptolemy's theory. Galileo was publicly honoured and returned triumphant. He then entered into some bitter arguments, including a dispute with a well-known Jesuit astronomer, Scheiner, about who first discovered sunspots. Later, Galileo disagreed with another Jesuit, Grassi, about comets. Unfortunately, some years later, an influential Jesuit was to be the Inquisition's Commissary General at Galileo's trial. Throughout his life Galileo skilfully poured scorn on those who disagreed with him. Even when his arguments were wrong, his tactics were very effective in making his opponents look small.

'... the scientist's vanity, quarrels over priority of discovery, contemptuous attitude and effective sarcasm cost him dearly in the long run'.

Dr Charles Hummel

Galileo and the Bible

In Galileo's day, Aristotle's and Ptolemy's ideas about physics and astronomy were accepted by professional philosophers. They saw disagreements as threatening their professional standing. In Rome, some Aristotelians, dubbed the 'Pigeon League', united to oppose Galileo, under the leadership of Colombe (meaning dove). He was a layman, from whom came the first opposition on religious grounds. He claimed various Bible texts taught the Earth was stationary. In 1615, Galileo wrote a long letter, 'Concerning the Use of Biblical Quotations in Matters of Science'. It was meant to answer theological objections to Copernicus' theory, cautioning the Roman Catholic Church against making particular views of astronomy matters of orthodox faith, since they might later be found wrong:

'... since the Holy Ghost did not intend to teach us whether heaven moves or stands still... nor whether the earth is located at its centre or off to one side, then so much the less was it intended to settle for us any other conclusion of the same kind... Now if the Holy Spirit has purposely neglected to teach us propositions of this sort as irrelevant to the highest goal (that is, to our salvation), how can anyone affirm that it is obligatory to take sides on them?... I should think it would be the part of prudence not to let anyone usurp scriptural texts and force them in some way to maintain any physical conclusion to be true, when at some future time the senses... may show the contrary.'

Instead, the letter stirred up trouble. Some church officials thought Galileo, a layman, was presumptuous for saying how to interpret the Bible. The Catholic Church was still smarting from the Reformation, a Europe-wide religious movement which challenged Papal authority by appealing directly to the Bible.

Galileo promised conclusive evidence for the Copernican system. Curiously, the best evidence lay, unrecognized, in a book on Galileo's shelf. Its author, Johannes Kepler, had sent it, in the year the telescope was invented, suggesting planets moved in ellipses, not circles.

Pope Paul V ordered an enquiry into how Copernicus' ideas compared with the Church's teaching. In 1616 the preliminary enquiry reported:

'[That] the sun is the centre of the world and completely immovable by local motion... was declared unanimously to be foolish and absurd in philosophy and formally heretical inasmuch as it expressly contradicts the doctrine of Holy Scripture in many passages, both in their literal meaning and according to the general interpretation of the Fathers and Doctors.'

Copernicus' book was temporarily suspended, pending a few minor changes, particularly to the preface. The Pope told Cardinal Bellarmine to persuade Galileo to abandon his views under threat of imprisonment. What actually happened when they met in 1616 is a mystery. Rumours began to circulate and Galileo asked Bellarmine for a written report of their meeting, to use in his own defence. The report said Galileo had not been forced to renounce his ideas on oath, or do penance. He had been told

> '... the doctrine of Copernicus, that the earth moves around the sun and that the sun is stationary in the centre of the universe and does not move from east to west, is contrary to Holy Scripture and therefore cannot be defended or held'.

For about seven years Galileo trod cautiously.

Galileo's Trial

On hearing news of the enthronement of a new Pope, a friend of Galileo, there was just time for Galileo to dedicate his latest book, *The Assayer*, to him before printing. Pope Urban VIII liked the book and Galileo travelled to Rome, hoping to have the ban on the Copernican system lifted. Galileo wanted to write another book called *Dialogue on the Flux and Reflux of the Tides*. He was convinced the tides provided concrete evidence for a moving earth, although Kepler said the Moon's attraction caused them.

The Pope insisted the treatment remain hypothetical, the title be changed to *Dialogue Concerning the Two Chief World Systems*, and his own 'unanswerable argument' be included. This was, since God could do anything, he could produce the tides how he liked and need not use the Earth's motion.

On publication, the book clearly did *not* treat the issues hypothetically; and there was a sting in the tail. The Pope's views were relegated to the end of the book and put into the mouth of Simplicio, whose name is a slight, but significant, change to that of an earlier commentator on Aristotle, called Simplicius. It translates as 'simpleton'!

The Pope, who had earlier written a poem in honour of Galileo, acted swiftly. A special commission was appointed and Galileo was summoned to Rome. In the Pope's words,

Galileo 'did not fear to make game of me'. During the period of his interrogation, Galileo lived in very comfortable apartments rather than dungeons. He was questioned about his earlier meeting with Cardinal Bellarmine (now dead) and minutes of that meeting were produced from the Vatican files; minutes unknown to Galileo, unsigned (which was irregular) and more strongly worded than Bellarmine's record. Recent examinations of the handwriting and the watermark of the paper show the minutes correspond with

Galileo Galilei before Pope Urban VIII in 1633. Engaving by Pardinel.

other documents in the file; so they do not appear to be a later forgery and the mystery remains.

Under questioning, Galileo claimed that he had not tried to defend Copernicus' views:

'I have neither maintained nor defended in that book the opinion that the earth moves and the sun is stationary, but have rather demonstrated the opposite of the Copernican opinion, and shown that the arguments of Copernicus are weak and not conclusive.'

This was outrageously untrue and could be seen to be so by anyone, like Galileo's inquisitors, who had read the book. The situation was ludicrous. Galileo's claim would never stand up in court. He also claimed to have forgotten what he had written and offered to add to the book to *disprove* the Copernican system more completely! A face-saving formula was needed and moves were made towards plea-bargaining and an out-of-court settlement.

Then came the bombshell. Almost certainly by order of the offended Pope came the command for Galileo to be interrogated under threat of torture. Though Galileo and his inquisitors knew the threat could not be carried out (it being illegal to torture a 70-year-old), it was an alarming turn of events. Four times, under oath, Galileo denied holding Copernican views. The intention was to humiliate him and to make him realize that he could not ride roughshod over the authorities without repercussions. Despite his anger, the Pope said that they would 'consult together so that he may suffer as little distress as possible'.

The trial stopped. Galileo was sentenced to read a recantation of his Copernican views, saying, 'with sincere heart and unfeigned faith I abjure, curse, and detest the aforesaid errors and heresies'. He was placed under house arrest, his prison initially being a rather sumptuous apartment at the Grand Duke's villa, then his own farm, and finally his own house in Florence. By permission, even the penance of daily reciting penitential Psalms was delegated to a nun, one of three children Galileo had had by his mistress.

'Although Galileo was not deeply spiritual, he was sincerely religious and a loyal churchman. The celebrated Galileo case, therefore, does not truly revolve about the perennial issues of science versus religion.'

Dr Raymond Seeger

Reflections on the Galileo Affair

Many attempts have been made to identify the key issues and why Galileo was treated harshly. Folklore often presents it as 'science versus religion'. But this is a simplistic view.

It did, however, concern issues of authority and freedom to publish. At various times Galileo had received support and encouragement from church leaders. However, a key factor was the highly sensitive issue of biblical interpretation in the wake of the 'Counter Reformation', the Roman Catholic Church's response to the Reformation. The Council of Trent

Giordano Bruno statue in Campo de Fiori, Rome.

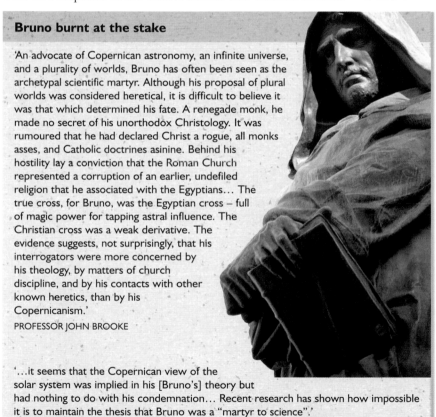

Bruno burnt at the stake

'An advocate of Copernican astronomy, an infinite universe, and a plurality of worlds, Bruno has often been seen as the archetypal scientific martyr. Although his proposal of plural worlds was considered heretical, it is difficult to believe it was that which determined his fate. A renegade monk, he made no secret of his unorthodox Christology. It was rumoured that he had declared Christ a rogue, all monks asses, and Catholic doctrines asinine. Behind his hostility lay a conviction that the Roman Church represented a corruption of an earlier, undefiled religion that he associated with the Egyptians... The true cross, for Bruno, was the Egyptian cross – full of magic power for tapping astral influence. The Christian cross was a weak derivative. The evidence suggests, not surprisingly, that his interrogators were more concerned by his theology, by matters of church discipline, and by his contacts with other known heretics, than by his Copernicanism.'

PROFESSOR JOHN BROOKE

'...it seems that the Copernican view of the solar system was implied in his [Bruno's] theory but had nothing to do with his condemnation... Recent research has shown how impossible it is to maintain the thesis that Bruno was a "martyr to science".'

PROFESSOR REIJER HOOYKAAS

decreed the ultimate authority for interpreting the Bible belonged to the Church Fathers. Galileo was presuming to interpret it himself in the light of the world around.

Sixteen years before Galileo's meeting with Cardinal Bellarmine, Giordano Bruno (1548–1600), a backslidden monk, had been burnt at the stake. In a book on the Eucharist, published in 1584, his references to the Copernican system were so badly wrong that the nonsense and huge errors might justly have earned him ridicule, but hardly persecution. But his cryptic writing embodied ideas the Roman Catholic Church saw as highly heretical.

When Galileo's book was published in 1632 it was, as in Bruno's time, a period of political and religious sensitivities between Spain, France and England. Pope Urban VIII had been accused of not being tough enough with trouble-makers, and at a meeting of cardinals that year, the one before Galileo's trial, he was verbally attacked by Cardinal Borgia (not the best of enemies!) for not giving enough support to the Spanish cause. Also, the ill-judged and ill-timed 'Simplicio' touch had deeply angered a Pope who already had more than enough problems on his plate. Perhaps these factors resulted in Urban VIII showing he could be tough, as a gesture towards his critics, tougher than might otherwise have been the case with someone who had once been a friend. Such comments do not excuse the appalling act of Bruno's execution, nor the treatment of Galileo. But they may help in understanding those causal factors that had few connections with a central sun.

So Galileo had argued for a heliocentric (approximately) universe, and the Roman Catholic Church for a geocentric one. But how does the controversy look from our present understanding of space–time? In the words of Professor Mary Hesse:

'There would now be almost universal agreement, first, that the Church sought to maintain an untenable doctrine of geocentrism that was quite unnecessary to its fundamental beliefs, and, second, that Galileo's theory, too, was mistaken, because we *would not now recognize any spatial point as the absolute centre of the universe, but would measure all positions and motions relatively to some point chosen for our own convenience.'*

But scientific ideas are constantly changing and future generations may view things differently. The twist in the story, according to Professor Giorgio de Santillana, is that:

'The views concerning the interpretation of Scripture contained in Galileo's theological letters have become the official doctrine of the [Roman Catholic] Church since Leo XIII's encyclical Providentissimus Deus *of 1893.'*

In summary of this chequered episode, with its faults on both sides:

'...Galileo can no longer be portrayed as the harbinger of truth and enlightenment who was pitted against reactionary priests who refused to look through the telescope. Instead he counted many Jesuits among his supporters, but his censure resulted partly from his mishandling of a sensitive diplomatic situation. The other paradigmatic conflict concerns the Darwinian theory of evolution...'

PROFESSOR GEOFFREY CANTOR

But that is the subject of chapter 9.

8. Enemies or Allies?

'... there have been apparent contradictions within science itself as formidable and difficult to resolve as any that have arisen between science and religion. Conflict between rival views is common in science'.

PROFESSOR MALCOLM DIXON

'Scientists are no more irreligious than other people. But the nature of their work concentrates their attention on questions of mechanism; and this very concentration tends to put out of focus questions of meaning.'

Professor Douglas Spanner

For centuries there have been fruitful interactions between science and religion, but also some controversies. As the Galileo affair shows, other major factors – social, cultural and personal – are often involved.

Einstein's religious views were idiosyncratic. He did not believe in a personal God. Richard Dawkins, in his recent book *The God Delusion*, usefully refers to 'Einsteinian religion' to distinguish it from 'supernatural religion'. But he then says, 'I suspect that most of the more recent ['Great scientists who profess religion'] are religious only in the Einsteinian sense... Nevertheless, there are some genuine specimens [*sic.*] of good scientists who are sincerely religious in the full, traditional sense', in Britain, and also in the United States. 'But, as in Britain, they stand out for their rarity and are a subject for amused bafflement to their peers in the academic community.'

This claim is quite astonishing. The people Dawkins refers to sound like collector's pieces! Actually, there are plenty of such academics and there are various learned societies for the study of science and religion to which hundreds of them belong. They are committed to serious examination of the points of interaction and to authoring scholarly publications. They would reject any suggestion that they were compartmentalizing their scientific and religious beliefs.

Returning to Einstein's position, one of his well-known quotations is: 'Science without religion is lame, religion without science is blind'; which raises the question, 'Does religion encourage science?' The answer seems to depend on the religious beliefs. The ancient Greeks' world-view was **organismic**, seeing the world as semi-divine. This did not help experimental work, since performing experiments on 'her' seemed rather like sacrilege. By contrast, one could cite Muslim pre-eminence in science for about 500 years from the mid-ninth century onwards. Also, there is the rapid development of science within the Western world during the sixteenth and seventeenth centuries. A **mechanistic** world-view had replaced the organismic one, highlighting the distinction between creator and creation, but also making problems of its own (p. 26). The dominant religion, Christianity, de-deified nature, and gave managerial responsibility to humankind.

> 'The world around us is not ours, God created it, and found that it was good, and to be enjoyed and protected. Humankind was given dominion over the rest of creation. "Dominion" means "lordship", implying caretaking, ownership or trusteeship, not wanton destruction.'

PROFESSOR SIR GHILLIAN PRANCE

Since understanding appeared to assist caretaking, science seemed to be encouraged. Furthermore, since God is a free agent, creation is **contingent** (it could have been otherwise), not **necessary**; so experiments were needed to find out how the world is, rather than how ancient wisdom thought it should be. Knowledge about the world could also help relieve suffering and show God's wisdom and power.

Above the oak door of the original Cavendish laboratory in Cambridge was carved the so-called 'research workers' text' from Psalm 111:2. Translated from the Latin it reads: 'The works of the Lord are great, sought out of all them that have pleasure therein.' The text, in English, is also over the entrance to the new Cavendish laboratory. Its first Professor of Experimental Physics, James Clerk Maxwell, wrote the following prayer.

'Sometimes people ask if religion and science are not opposed to one another. They are: in the sense that the thumb and fingers of my hand are opposed to one another. It is an opposition by means of which anything can be grasped.'

Professor Sir William Bragg

*'...teach us to study the works of Thy hands that we may subdue
the earth to our use, and strengthen our reason for Thy service'.*

The Search for Independence

The partnership of Christianity with science was commonly
accepted until the last decades of the nineteenth century.
Many clergy were scientists, and their understanding of the
world deepened their faith rather than destroyed it.
Subsequently, it was not simply that new scientific
discoveries (for example, evolution and the Earth's age)
raised questions about Christian beliefs. Many of the new
breed of professional scientists wanted to conduct their
science without reference to the church, seeing science as
offering more important knowledge. Behind the science and
religion debates of the nineteenth century was a struggle for
intellectual and cultural independence.

In some cases science and religion have deliberately been
portrayed as enemies. One group of nine famous Victorian
scientists, eight of them Fellows of the Royal Society, banded
together into a group called the 'X-Club'. They shared an
anti-clerical attitude, declaring that 'the bond that united us
was devotion to science, pure and free, untrammelled by
religious dogmas'.

*'The movement spawned by the X-Club and its sympathizers has
been called "Victorian scientific naturalism". In its simplest form
this was a concerted attempt to replace conventional religion...
by a world-view that involves nature and nature only. Its aim
was the secularization of society... the church (that is, the
Established Church) had to be discredited... deliberately or in
ignorance, three centuries of alliance between Christianity and
science were quickly forgotten and a new mythology engineered...*

*'A whole new literature emerged as "history" was rewritten,
literature that today is almost universally regarded as worthless
for any true insights into the close historical interactions
between religion and science... scholars are still having to live
with an enduring mythology which has etched itself deeply into*

the national consciousness, precisely as intended.
'In attacking the church, "Mother Nature" was an
indispensable ally. She was, in short, a substitute for God...'
PROFESSOR COLIN RUSSELL

'Old Mother Nature' still gets vested with the ability to think, plan and organize. Even today, the oddity of crediting *nature* (everything), with *creating* everything, seems to escape notice! Other concepts, encountered later, also get personified and treated similarly.

Five historians of science comment on the 'conflict' view of science and religion

'The old model of inevitable conflict (still visible in the writings of extremists on either side) has been heavily qualified, if not abandoned.'
PROFESSOR PETER BOWLER

'... what nineteenth-century rationalist historians liked to call the warfare between science and religion... that popular but simplistic formula'.
PROFESSOR JOHN BROOKE

'The various forms of the conflict thesis have attracted much support, but they are not adequate as general claims about how science and religion have been interrelated in history. To extend the military metaphor, the conflict thesis is like a great blunderbuss which obliterates the fine texture of history and sets science and religion in necessary and irrevocable opposition. Much historical research has invalidated the conflict thesis...'
PROFESSOR GEOFFREY CANTOR

'Hitherto ignorance has played as significant a part as propaganda in perpetuating this mirage... I do not mean to say, of course, that there have never been confrontations between the ecclesiastical hierarchy and the advocates of science. My point is that the conflict model is a particularly crude tool for reconstructing the historical relationship between science and faith.'
PROFESSOR DAVID LIVINGSTONE

'... to portray them [science and religion] as persistently in conflict is not only historically inaccurate, but actually a caricature so grotesque that what needs to be explained is how it could possibly have achieved any degree of respectability'.
PROFESSOR COLIN RUSSELL

Limitations of Science

Another reason for the persistence of a 'warfare' model is the failure to recognize the limitations of science, sometimes as a consequence of earlier bad science education.

Some people have demanded 'scientific proof that God exists'; an odd request since science only deals with the natural world and God is not a material thing. Religion, however, includes questions as to whether there is anything other than the natural world (i.e. God), to which the natural world owes its existence; and it is no use going to science, the study of the natural world, to find out if there is anything other than the natural world. So Richard Dawkins' reassertion, in *The God Delusion*, that God is 'a scientific hypothesis', has a strange ring to it, as did his earlier claim, confirmed in our written debate,[6] that he pays 'religions the

Logical positivism

The view that science gave 'certain' or 'positive' knowledge through the senses was adopted by a group of philosophers, the Vienna Circle, in the 1920s/30s. By applying logic they claimed to have constructed a theory about what could meaningfully be said, calling it logical positivism. Professor Bertrand Russell summarized its claims:

'Whatever knowledge is attainable, must be attained by scientific methods; and what science cannot discover, mankind cannot know.'

If science could lead us into all truth, then since it only deals with material things it would necessarily follow that only material things existed! This imperialistic view of science exalted it to a golden image, dismissing religious, ethical and metaphysical statements as meaningless.

But few philosophers now support it. It proves fatal to science itself, on whose foundation it claimed to have been built! Professor Sir Karl Popper, philosopher of science, exposed a fatal weakness: 'positivists, in their anxiety to annihilate metaphysics, annihilate natural science along with it', since science itself involves presuppositions (pp. 7–8), which cannot be verified by sensory experience! The much-vaunted Verification Principle failed to meet its own demands. Logical positivism, like relativism, turned out to be self-referentially incoherent; it 'shot itself in the foot' and since the golden image, like that in the book of Daniel, had feet partly of clay, they shattered.

compliment of regarding them as scientific theories'. It might be asked what professional philosopher would support such a claim?

The limitations of science lie not so much in the territory it explores, for all the natural world is in principle open to scientific study; but rather in the methods it uses, the questions it can answer and the types of explanations it gives. Science can deal with spectral wavelengths, but not the beauty of a sunset; with pair-bonding, but not love. Furthermore, science cannot tell us whether courses of action are right or wrong, only what are their likely consequences.

'*Scientism*'

When distinctive extra beliefs are attached to science – metaphysical ones such as atheism or the omnicompetence of science – the letters 'ism' are often added, indicating system-building or special theories. Giving to science the false image of being the source of all truth and free from error is 'Scientism', not science, an image some advertisers promote; if it is 'new' as well, that is better still! 'New' reminds us that the content of science changes, as does the philosophy of science. Science is 'unfinished business'; there is no absolute certainty of having reached true understanding.

There has sometimes been a tendency towards arrogance about science when awe, wonder and humility would be more appropriate – qualities singularly lacking in one of the evolution 'debates' featured in the next section.

'I do not know what I may appear to the world; but to myself I seem to have been only like a boy playing on the sea-shore, and diverting myself in now and then finding a smoother pebble or a prettier shell than ordinary, while the great ocean of truth lay all undiscovered before me.'
SIR ISAAC NEWTON

9. *Creation and Evolution*

'The most persistent misapprehension about God and creation, however, is that knowledge of causal mechanism automatically excludes any possibility that God is acting in a particular situation.'

Professor Sam Berry

Some religious believers get worried by evolution, thinking it displaces God; some atheists get over-enthusiastic, imagining it justifies atheism.

- **Creation**, theologically, is God's act of bringing-and-sustaining-in-being. The word 'creation' gets borrowed and applied to new objects, ideas and fashions.

- **Evolution** is a process, known from family resemblances long before Charles Darwin, who preferred 'descent with modification'.

Representing an **act** as an alternative to a **process** makes a category mistake, like insisting on choosing between 'red' and 'noisy'. 'Red' is a colour; 'noisy', a sound. They are not logical alternatives. Cars can be both red and noisy!

'We were *created* by God or we came about by *evolution*' sounds reasonable until we compare a similar sentence: 'This car was *created* by the design team or it came about by

automation'. Automation is the process the agents (design team) used in creating the car; evolution can be the process the agent (God) used in creating us.

Evolution (accepted by biologists) and the mechanisms of change (still debated) need distinguishing. Darwin suggested a plausible mechanism with supporting evidence, some of which was collected between 1831–36 as 'gentleman companion' to Captain Fitzroy of *HMS Beagle*, sailing to improve the Admiralty charts of South America's coastline.

Articles Darwin took with him on HMS Beagle.

DARWIN KNEW THAT:

1. Living things reproduce freely in the wild, resulting in competition for food and space.

2. Animals prey on each other.

3. Offspring are not exactly like their parents.

4. Many characteristics are inherited, though Darwin had no idea how.

5. Longer-living members of species are likely to reproduce most.

DARWIN'S THEORY WAS THAT:

- Some variations, like longer legs, camouflage, different-shaped beaks and woolly coats, give better chances of survival against predators, food shortage and cold, so these variants live longer.

- If 4 and 5 (see above) are true, more will come to possess such characteristics.

Darwin's thinking was influenced by **artificial selection** used for breeding pigeons, racehorses and dogs. Owners only bred animals with desirable characteristics. By analogy, said Darwin, 'The preservation of favourable individual differences and variations, and the destruction of those which are injurious, I have called Natural Selection.'

Darwin was also impressed by a book by Thomas Malthus, an Anglican clergyman. Malthus argued that, because populations tend to increase faster than available food supplies, there will always be a struggle for existence. Long afterwards Darwin wrote:

'It at once struck me that under these circumstances favourable variations would tend to be preserved and unfavourable ones to be destroyed. The result of this would be the formation of a new species. Here, then, I had at last got a theory by which to work.'

In captivity, artificial selection was clear; but could it work in the wild? Why did heritable characteristics not die out by dilution? Darwin reasoned from a theory of blending inheritance, genes being unknown. Mating between pairs, one having a particular characteristic and the other not, was expected to result in each offspring having a reduced amount, like mixing clean water with red ink to give a pink liquid.

Twentieth-century genetics, after a bad start, produced a New Synthesis (called Neo-Darwinism). Mating was eventually compared to mixing two heaps of variously coloured counters, representing genes. The 'offspring' either contain particular coloured counters or do not. If the genetic information produces offspring better fitted to survive and reproduce, the genes get carried into future generations. This seems straightforward enough, so why any religious unease?

Before his voyage, Darwin held the widely-accepted belief that God

Darwin's religious beliefs

Darwin was reticent about these, saying, '... my judgment often fluctuates... In my most extreme fluctuations I have never been an Atheist in the sense of denying the existence of a God, I think that generally (and more and more as I grow older), but not always, that an Agnostic would be the more correct description of my state of mind.'

Popular biographies often claim Darwin gave up his beliefs because of science. But he was already rejecting Christianity, finding hell unpalatable, doubting the Bible and rejecting miracles. But according to some historians, the death of his favourite child, Annie, did most damage.

created different species separately, with characteristics suited to their environments; for example, giraffes had long necks to reach food. Within species, individual differences were usually small; hybrids were generally sterile. It seemed unlikely that species could change into others, an idea seemingly supported by one reading of Genesis (p. 15). During the voyage, said Darwin, 'vague doubts occasionally flitted across my mind' regarding whether species were fixed. Later he wrote: 'I am almost convinced (quite contrary to the opinion I started with) that species are not (it is like confessing to a murder) immutable.'

Various imaginative attempts were made, one by Archbishop Ussher of Armagh (1581–1656), to date the Earth from incomplete chronologies in Genesis. The resulting 4004 BCE was printed in the margins of some copies of the Bible, giving it a spurious air of orthodoxy and authority. Charles Lyell, Darwin's friend, and a number of

Joseph Hooker (1817–1911), Charles Lyell (1797–1875) and Charles Darwin (1809–1882).

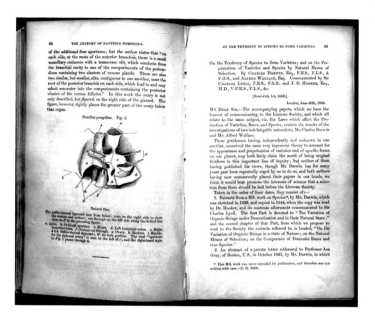

Linnean Society proceedings for 1 July 1858.

other eminent geologists, thought the evidence pointed to a much older Earth. If so, Darwin argued, over longer periods many small changes within a species might add up to big ones, species possibly evolving into others. Lyell was initially against this view.

Darwin wrote out a short version of his 'species theory' in 1842. Lyell urged him to publish, lest he be pre-empted, but Darwin wanted more time. In June 1858 Darwin heard from Alfred Wallace, a fellow naturalist in Malaya, who had had similar ideas and wanted help in getting them published. Darwin wrote to Lyell: 'Your words have come true with a vengeance – that I should be forestalled... I never saw a more striking coincidence: if Wallace had my MS. sketch written out in 1842, he could not have made a better short abstract!'

Lyell and other friends quickly arranged for extracts from Wallace's paper and one by Darwin to be read at the Linnean Society. Little interest was shown. The annual Presidential report said 'The year... has not been marked by any of those striking discoveries which revolutionize the department of science on which they bear'!

The pressure was on Darwin to publish. A substantial volume, *The Origin of Species*, appeared the following year, challenging the fixity of species. Humans were hardly mentioned, but the obvious implications were developed in Darwin's book, *The Descent of Man*, published in 1871.

Impact of The Origin of Species

Folklore says Darwin's theory was welcomed by scientists and opposed by the religious. But many scientists were religious, presenting difficulties for this view.

'One writer states flatly that "many theologians and a few scientists rejected the hypothesis outright as 'the latest form of infidelity'". The truth is nearer to the exact opposite: it was a few theologians and many scientists who dismissed Darwinism and evolution.'

PROFESSOR JAMES MOORE

First edition of
The Origin of
Species
*published in
November 1859
(1,250 copies).*

Darwin and others knew of good scientific reasons for not accepting his theory. Darwin listed them and sought answers. Samuel Wilberforce, Bishop of Oxford and third son of William Wilberforce, highlighted many in a review of the *Origin* that Darwin called 'uncommonly clever; it picks out with skill all the most conjectural parts, and brings forward well all the difficulties'. The Bishop, though much maligned, was no ignoramus. He had an Oxford Mathematics First and was Vice-President of the British Association for the Advancement of Science (BAAS). His review consisted almost entirely of scientific criticisms, belying the popular image of an obscurantist clergyman opposing science:

'We have objected to the views with which we are dealing solely on scientific grounds... We have no sympathy with those who object to any facts or alleged facts in nature... because they believe them to contradict what it appears to them is taught by Revelation. We think that all such objections savour of a timidity which is really inconsistent with a firm and well-intrusted faith.'

'Much ado about...'?

The two protagonists in the Oxford 'debate':

LEFT: Samuel Wilberforce, Bishop of Oxford. From The Illustrated London News, *26 July 1873.*

RIGHT: Thomas Henry Huxley, biologist. Huxley was known as Darwin's bulldog because of his ardent support of Darwin's theory of evolution. From The Popular Science Review *London, April 1866.*

On 30 June 1860, a 'legendary encounter' took place in Oxford between Bishop Wilberforce and Thomas Henry Huxley. A crowd of 700 attended a BAAS lecture given by an American, Professor Draper, on 'the intellectual development of Europe with reference to the views of Mr Darwin and others...'. Charles Darwin was absent through ill health. The Bishop, whose review would shortly appear, was expected to speak; hence the crowd. It seemed likely that his critique of Darwin's theory would carry the day. Circumstances, however, altered this. Professor Draper spoke at length on a hot summer's day and the audience became restive. Huxley, who planned to be absent, was persuaded to attend. Wilberforce made some ill-judged humorous aside or social gaffe. Referring to an earlier comment in the BAAS meetings, he seems to have asked whether Huxley was related by his grandfather's or grandmother's side to an ape. Huxley was stung into action. His outlook was anti-clerical. Not being a practising member of the Church of England, Huxley was ineligible for Oxford and Cambridge and found difficulty in getting employment. Records of what followed are scarce and vary in reliability. Two months later Huxley wrote what he

thought he had said:

> 'If then, said I, the question is put to me would I rather have a miserable ape for a grandfather or a man highly endowed by nature and possessed of great means and influence and yet who employs those faculties for the mere purpose of introducing ridicule into a grave scientific discussion – I unhesitatingly affirm my preference for the ape.'

Oxford University Museum of Natural History, scene of the 'debate' between Wilberforce and Huxley.

By contrast, Joseph Hooker, Assistant Director of Kew Gardens, wrote to Darwin a few days later saying Huxley 'could not throw his voice over so large an assembly, nor command the audience'. Hooker's contribution was more prominently reported in one journal than Huxley's or Wilberforce's. *The Athenaeum* (7 July 1860) said that Huxley, Wilberforce and a few others 'have each found foemen worthy of their steel, and made their charges and countercharges very much to their own satisfaction and the delight of their respective friends'.

The discussions, including Bishop Wilberforce's contribution, had been largely about scientific difficulties over Darwin's theory. But a bishop entering the debate provided those who later wished to portray the encounter as 'science versus religion' with the ammunition they craved.

> 'It is a significant fact that the famous clash between Huxley and the Bishop was not reported by a single London newspaper at the time, and that of the few weekly reviews that mentioned it none brought out the force of Huxley's remark.'
> PROFESSOR ALVAR ELLEGARD

After the dust settled, the encounter attracted little written reference for the next 20 years. In 1860, the establishment was more shaken by the theologically liberal publication, *Essays and Reviews*. But after that long gap the

Wilberforce–Huxley exchange was disinterred, rewritten and exaggerated to become iconic, another symbolic myth like the Galileo affair for those wishing to promulgate a view of science in necessary conflict with religion. Furthermore the sermon, *The Present Relations of Science to Religion*, preached before the University of Oxford by Frederick Temple (later Archbishop of Canterbury) on the day following the encounter, gets conveniently forgotten. As the quotation on page 10 indicates, Temple's assessment of advances in science was more positive than fits the legend.

Such stories are popular in media presentations since confrontations like these increase viewing ratings; sadly, too, in some educational resources. They are difficult to dislodge, and the scarcity of historical detail gives scope for fertile imaginations to run riot. So, was the encounter 'a storm in a Victorian teacup'? Professor Cantor gives a demythologizing summary of the Wilberforce–Huxley confrontation:

> 'These opponents are now viewed as trading minor insults in the heat of debate and not as exemplifying the necessary conflict between science and religion. Moreover, in the latter nineteenth century Darwinian theory was not generally seen as antagonistic to scriptural religion.'

When *The Origin of Species* was published, some Christians welcomed it as a further step in tracing God's creative work. Professor James Moore comments, 'With but few exceptions the leading Christian thinkers in both Great Britain and America came to terms quite readily with both Darwinism and evolution.'

So, too, with the age of the Earth:

> '... by and large, Christian geologists had both encountered and accommodated the issue of the age of the earth long before the appearance of Darwin's theory'.
> PROFESSOR DAVID LIVINGSTONE

Young-Earth Creationism

Thus it was surprising to find renewed belief in a young Earth, initially through the influences of Ellen White (1827–1915), a Seventh-day Adventist prophetess, and her young Canadian disciple, George McCready Price (1870–1963). In 1961 *The Genesis Flood* by Henry Morris (Professor of Hydraulic Engineering) and John Whitcomb Jr. (Professor of Old Testament) appeared in the US, written in a similar vein.

> **A tongue-in-cheek comment!**
>
> 'With the Lord a day is like a thousand years, and a thousand years are like a day' (2 Peter 3:8). It has been pointed out that this involves a ratio of 365,000:1. Orthodox views of Earth's age, compared with young-Earth creationism, give the similar ratio of 460,000:1.

Young-Earth creationists read Genesis in a particular way, as Special Creations during a week of sudden, all-powerful miracles some 10,000 years ago. Despite being at variance with the 4.6 thousand million years of mainstream cosmology, geology, physics and biology, substantial investment in resources has resulted in 'young-Earth' views gaining a considerable following.

Long before evidence for an ancient Earth was available, early Church Fathers such as Augustine interpreted the 'days' of Genesis differently. It was not that new meanings arose simply because of nineteenth-century discoveries in geology. Origen, writing in c. 225 CE wrote:

> 'What man of intelligence, I ask, will consider as a reasonable statement that the first and the second and the third day, in which there are said to be both morning and evening, existed without sun and moon and stars, while the first day was even without a heaven?'

Origen knew, as did others, that '24-hour' days with mornings and evenings were meaningless before the Sun and other stars were created on day four. St Augustine (354–430 CE) was even more outspoken:

'Usually, even a non-Christian knows something about the earth, the heavens, and the other elements of this world... Now, it is a disgraceful and dangerous thing for an infidel to hear a Christian, presumably giving the meaning of Holy Scripture, talking nonsense on these topics... people outside of the household of the faith think our sacred writers held such opinions, and... If they find a Christian mistaken in a field which they themselves know well and hear him maintaining his foolish opinions about our books, how are they going to believe those books in matters concerning the resurrection of the dead, the hope of eternal life, and the kingdom of heaven...?'

Tough talk! But it is thought-provoking that the results of one study 'confirm the findings... among 16 to 18-year-olds that both scientism and the perception of Christianity as necessarily involving creationism... contribute to making it more difficult for pupils to combine a positive attitude towards Christianity with a high level of interest in science'.

The term 'Creationism'

Christians, Muslims and Orthodox Jews, and others who believe God created everything, can properly be called 'creationists'. They may accept evolutionary processes, which those who annexed the label 'creationist' deny. But if extra beliefs about creation, concerning mode or age are imported, new terms are appropriate. Old-Earth creationism, progressive creationism and young-Earth creationism are such terms. But the abbreviated term 'creationism' has become associated in the public mind with young-Earth creationism since about 1980.

Some people, unsympathetic to religion, mistakenly imagine that showing the inadequacies of creationist biology and geology disproves not only young-Earth creationism but creation as well, causing further confusion.

Evolution, like creation, tends to attract extra beliefs that do not follow from biology, resulting in evolutionism.

> **'I would venture to say, and it breaks my heart to say so, that more damage has been done to the image of Christian faith amongst our non-believer colleagues by the extreme views of the young-earth creationist movement than by any other group, despite their sincerity.'**
>
> *Professor Francis Collins*

Evolutionism

'... much of the energy of the creationist movement arises from a sense of moral outrage at the advance of an evolution-centred world-view that has the audacity to parade its secular, liberal values as if they were the objective findings of science. Here at least, if not in matters of biological fact and theory, creationism has a point of which the scientific community might do well to take heed.'

PROFESSOR JOHN DURANT

The forms these 'extra beliefs' take are:

1. REIFICATION
Concepts such as evolution, nature, chance and natural selection get treated like 'things' that can 'create', 'choose', 'build' and cause events. Reification (from the Latin *res* meaning 'thing') is the fallacy of confusing a concept with an object or a cause. Claiming evolution is the *cause* of our being here, instead of a generalization about descent with modification, is committing this fallacy. Sloppy talk like 'It wasn't God; evolution did it' is sometimes used to disparage plan or purpose in creation. But evolution does not justify this, although both evolution and science sometimes seem to get treated as 'crutches for atheism'. But atheism is not a necessary consequence of either; and claims that it is gives science an undeservedly bad name. Darwin pointed out in a letter written on his behalf: 'He considers that the theory of evolution is quite compatible with the belief in a God; but that you must remember that different persons have different definitions of what they mean by God.'

2. PROGRESS
'Progress' is not an isolated word, but is always towards some desired goal. Herbert Spencer (1820–1903), a member of the Victorian X-Club, sought to popularize evolution, applying its principles to society. He coined the ambiguous term 'survival of the fittest'. Apparently a

Poster from the exhibition 'Deadly Medicine: Creating the Master Race'. The exhibition shows how doctors implemented the order Hitler signed on September 1, 1939 to kill the fatally ill and the handicapped. It traces in detail the fate of the first victims of Hitler's sinister 'health' policies, based on his obsession with racial purity that led to the Holocaust. The poster reads 'There will be a drop in the quality of the population if high-value people fail to reproduce sufficiently – and that will happen if sub-standard people have four children and high-value people only have two.'

tautology – the 'fittest' are 'those who survive' – 'fittest' is now assigned a different meaning:

> ' "The survival of the fittest" no longer implies a gladiatorial view of nature, for survival now means reproductive success; not the conqueror, but the parent with the largest number of progeny reaching parenthood, is the fittest.'
>
> PROFESSOR IAN BARBOUR

Victorian Capitalism thrived on industrial competition and tried to justify cut-throat competition in business using evolution. Communism enlisted biological struggle to incite violent revolution. Both claimed support from evolution, as did Nazism. Three such disparate ideologies cannot all logically follow from the same scientific theory. The idea of struggle was overplayed and aspects of evolution that contradicted their beliefs were neglected. Tennyson's poem 'In Memoriam', published a few years before the *Origin*, spoke of 'Nature, red in tooth and claw'. His words were an overstatement, at a time when biology was less understood. There are many other relationships between individuals, including **symbiosis**, in which organisms depend on each other, and **altruism**, in which individuals die for other members of their species.

These ideologies could only claim scientific backing if biology showed what we ought to do. It cannot. Attempts to derive 'evolutionary ethics' fall into the is/ought fallacy. There is no valid route from how the world is, to what ought to be done; some moral dimension has to be added. Competition in nature does not justify cut-throat business practices, violent revolutions or gas chambers. But because Hitler appealed to the 'survival of the fittest' for his 'master race', evolution has been called evil. Like the claim that religion is bad because evil things have been done in its name (pp. 26–29), this too is a bad argument. Misuse does not necessarily make something bad in itself. Nobel's invention of dynamite rendered nitroglycerine, an unstable explosive, safe for quarrying. But Nobel was horrified to see how dynamite was being misused and gave some of his fortune to establish the Nobel Peace Prize.

Human moral progress is not entailed by evolution:

> 'The types which survive are deemed to be valuable by no criterion other than the fact of their survival.'
> PROFESSOR C.E.M. JOAD

An obituary of Sir Julian Huxley said he came 'to treat evolutionism as a sort of secular religion'. Writing at that time from a secularist viewpoint, the philosopher, Professor Anthony Flew criticized Huxley for his attempt to derive evolutionary ethics:

> 'There is, surely, something very odd, indeed pathetic, in Huxley's attempt to find in evolutionary biology "something, not ourselves, which makes for righteousness". For this quest is for him a search for something, not God, which does duty for Divine Providence. Yet if there really is no Divine Providence operating in the universe, then indeed there is none; and we cannot reasonably expect to find in the Godless workings of impersonal things those comfortable supports which – however mistakenly – believers usually think themselves entitled to derive from their theistic beliefs.'

Huxley was not alone in adding extra beliefs to evolution, and the philosopher Dr Mary Midgley gave many examples in *Evolution as a Religion: Strange hopes and stranger fears*, which was dedicated 'To the Memory of Charles Darwin Who Did Not Say These Things'.

Biology and behaviour

Courses of action are sometimes claimed as right because they are 'natural'. But though the word 'natural' is used approvingly about foods (not about mosquitoes or poison ivy), what is natural is not necessarily good or morally right. It may be natural to hit someone back, but not right. It is natural to want sex; but not right for a man to take any woman he fancies.

Human behaviour is affected by heredity and environment: by **nature** through genes; by **nurture** through upbringing. But we are not bound by natural selection; we may go against it. Weak and aged people are not exterminated, but are often cared for. Humans may control their development and environment, rather than being carried helplessly along. Not everyone agrees about freedom of choice. Sociology, in an extreme form, may claim, not simply that we are influenced by nature or nurture, but that we are completely determined by them. But is this claim also determined?

Sociobiology, especially associated with E.O. Wilson's name, claims that all behaviour is determined by genes and reproductive advantage, looking to genetics for explanations of all social behaviour. Wilson accommodates religious behaviour by asserting, 'The highest forms of religious practice, when examined more closely, can be seen to confer biological advantage.' He also maintains: 'The final decisive edge enjoyed by scientific naturalism will come from its capacity to explain traditional religion, its chief competitor, as a wholly material phenomenon.' Professor Trigg, however, points out the following inconsistency: 'The sociobiological explanation of religion seems to try to show why religious belief is held even though it is false.' But, he goes on to say, 'If

Wilson's view of religion is correct, a major decline in religious commitment would be biologically harmful, and yet it appears that sociobiology is encouraging this.'

Creation, Risk and Theodicy

Creating a material and populated world also brings into being problems and risks for us and, in a different way, for God. As with architects who have chosen their building materials, the materials God has created result in the following:

Constraints on how creation functions

• According to current science, matter arising from the Big Bang collected under gravity, forming stars. From these came the elements making up our bodies, plus a lot of residual radiation and particles everywhere.

• The residual radiation produces mutations in living matter, some of which are harmful and others not. Mutations result in utility and beauty in the rich diversity of life; and ugliness in the cancers that attack our bodies. This is termed the free process aspect of suffering.

• Gravity results in the birth and death of stars, in matter having weight and us remaining on Earth; but heavy bodies can kill. Apparently undeserved suffering has troubled people since antiquity. The Mosaic law made provision for accidental killing: 'For instance, a man may go into the forest with his neighbour to cut wood, and as he swings his axe to fell a tree, the head may fly off and hit his neighbour and kill him. That man may flee to one of these cities [of refuge] and save his life' (Deuteronomy 19:5). Jesus responded to a first-century tragedy, saying 'those eighteen who died when the tower in Siloam fell on them – do you think they were more guilty than all the others living in Jerusalem?' (Luke 13:4).

• The mass of molten rock that became our Earth contracts on cooling, producing earthquakes.

- The vast oceans maintain temperatures that permit human and other life (p. 77). But large underwater earthquakes can result in tsunamis. The affluent West has some early warning systems; poorer countries bordering the Indian Ocean did not, as seen on Boxing Day 2004.

- Sensitivity to pain is necessary to alert us to dangers and bodily problems that need attention.

But this protecting mechanism also leads to pain and suffering in accidents, illness and dying.

Justifying God's goodness in such a world is the subject matter of **theodicy**. This was of agonizing concern to Darwin when Annie, his ten-year-old daughter, died. So, too, for C.S. Lewis who, after writing a balanced consideration of *The Problem of Pain*, graphically described his emotional trauma at the premature death of his wife Joy, in *A Grief Observed*.

A common response to tragedy is to ask, 'Why couldn't God have made a better job of creation; God is supposed to be able to do anything, isn't he?' This is easy to ask but realistic alternatives are rarely suggested.

The film *Bruce Almighty* (2003) made some serious points about constraints and free will in a telling and often controversial way. Bruce, a television news reporter, finds his world falling to pieces and complains to God. God gives him almighty powers for a time to try to run the world better, with the proviso 'you can't mess with free will'. Initially Bruce uses his powers like a conjuror, selfishly causing chaos. A whimsical desire to have a closer moon causes a tsunami. He becomes painfully aware of the free will constraint in a fluctuating relationship with his girlfriend, attempting to override her free will, crying 'Love me, love me, love me!' In desperation he asks, 'How do you make someone love you without affecting free will?'

The problem of evil is sometimes put in a rather slick form: some say that God cannot be all-powerful and all-good. If he wants to stop evil, but cannot, he cannot be all-powerful: if he is all-powerful, but does not stop it, he cannot be all-

'... meaningless combinations of words do not suddenly acquire meaning simply because we prefix to them the two other words "God can"...

It is no more possible for God than for the weakest of his creatures to carry out both of two mutually exclusive alternatives; not because His power meets an obstacle, but because nonsense remains nonsense even when we talk it about God.'

Professor C.S. Lewis

good. As a piece of rhetoric it trips neatly off the tongue, but it fails to do justice to logical constraints. If love is to be a prime value, there must be free choice. To speak of forcing someone to love is a contradiction in terms. A creator who desires creatures involved in a loving relationship, has to give freedom not to love. That is God's risk – the free will aspect of suffering. God's 'heartache', trying to woo back his rebellious people Israel, is movingly described in the Old Testament by the prophet Hosea. Jesus Christ's anguish is poignantly expressed, through a maternal metaphor, as he weeps over Jerusalem, saying, 'how often I have longed to gather your children together, as a hen gathers her chicks under her wings, but you were not willing!' (Luke 13:34). To ask, 'Why doesn't God create people who have to love him?' is therefore meaningless.

Much evil results from human sin, most obviously when we think of wars, selfishness and greed rather than natural disasters; but even here there may be human failing – say, through not taking global warming seriously. Two words the Bible uses for 'sin' mean 'transgression' and 'missing the mark'. The first refers to active disobedience, crossing forbidden boundaries, *sins of commission*. The second indicates falling short of some standard, *sins of omission*. People have speculated whether part of the original command to subdue the Earth may have involved controlling natural forces, perhaps as the synoptic writers record Jesus doing with the storm on Lake Galilee (Matthew 8:23–27). But we simply do not know what the world would have been like if sin had not entered. The apostle Paul describes creation as 'groaning as in the pains of childbirth' (Romans 8:22). Furthermore, human failure apart, the Bible also speaks of spiritual powers of wickedness.

'Therefore I am now going to allure her; I will lead her into the desert and speak tenderly to her. There I will give her back her vineyards, and will make the Valley of Achor a door of hope. There she will sing as in the days of her youth, as in the day she came up out of Egypt.'

Hosea 2.14–15

10. Accident or Design?

Arguments from Design

The mathematician and theologian William Paley (1743–1805) said that finding a stone on a heath would have

no significance but finding a watch, designed for a purpose, would. By analogy, he argued that creatures apparently fitted for their environment also suggested a designer. Originally impressed by Paley, Darwin later wrote:

'The old argument from design in Nature, as given by Paley, which formerly seemed to me so conclusive, fails, now that the law of natural selection has been discovered.'

Certainly, evolution by natural selection replaced numerous separate creations, but these were not necessarily implied by the biblical accounts anyway. Darwin's closing words of the *Origin* portrayed evolution from various forms as fitting for God's activity:

'There is grandeur in this view of life, with its separate powers, having been originally breathed by the Creator into a few forms or into one... from so simple a beginning endless forms most beautiful and most wonderful have been and are being evolved.'

However, some saw Darwin's metaphor of natural selection portraying design as weeding out living things less fitted for survival and reproduction. This seemed wasteful, involving suffering and death (pp. 107–109). So it was not so much evolution but Darwin's mechanism of natural selection that was distasteful to many in Victorian society. Nevertheless, Darwin's own comparison of human selection and natural selection could imply that intelligence works through nature, much as intelligence worked through pigeon breeding. Darwin conceded in a letter:

> '*I can see no reason why a man, or other animal, may not have been expressly designed by an omniscient Creator, who foresaw every future event and consequence.*'

In one way it is odd that evolution should have caused religious objections. Charles Kingsley, author of *The Water Babies*, enthused over Darwin's theory, saying: 'they find that now they have got rid of an interfering God [p. 57] – a master-magician, as I call it – they have to chose between the absolute empire of accident, and a living, immanent, ever-working God'. For any theory of God's 'occasional intervention' would also imply his 'ordinary absence'.

Darwin included an extract of a letter from Kingsley in the *Origin*, saying: 'A celebrated author and divine has written to me that "he has gradually learnt to see that it is just as noble a conception of the Deity to believe that He created a few original forms capable of self-development into other and needful forms, as to believe that he required a fresh act of creation to supply the voids caused by the action to His laws".'

Evolution by natural selection does mean that available ecological niches are likely to be occupied. So provided changes in climate and food supplies are not too rapid, populations can adapt, rather than dying out. Frederick Temple (pp. 10, 100) argued:

> '*What is touched by this doctrine [of Evolution] is not the evidence of design but the mode in which the design was executed... In the one case the Creator made the animals at once such as they now are; in the other case He impressed on certain*

> *particles of matter... such inherent powers that in the ordinary course of time living creatures such as the present were developed... He did not make the things, we may say; no, but He made them make themselves.'*

In denying a world that is designed, Professor Richard Dawkins has coined the word 'designoid' to refer to what he regards as 'an object that LOOKS good enough for it to have been designed, but which in fact has grown up by an entirely different process, an automatic, unguided and wholly unthought-out process'. This comment raises a further matter.

The functional integrity of creation

One meaning of the word 'integrity' is 'completeness'. Genesis

describes creation as 'good', as fit for purpose. The functional integrity of creation speaks of an inbuilt capability to operate, upheld by the creator. Mark's Gospel illustrates this:

> *'A man scatters seed on the ground... the seed sprouts and grows, though he does not know how. All by itself [from the Greek automatos] the soil produces corn — first the stalk, then the ear, then the full grain in the ear.'*
> MARK 4:26–28

In saying 'All by itself', Mark most certainly was not presenting seed-germination as 'unguided and wholly unthought-out'.

Failure to recognize the integrity of creation led to the explanatory confusion, the 'God-of-the-gaps' (pp. 33–35). This idea currently seems to be experiencing revival in the following movement.

The Intelligent Design (ID) Movement

It is claimed that intelligence in creation is shown by **irreducible complexity** in nature. Michael Behe explains this term using a mousetrap as an example, meaning that it will not work (i.e. catch mice) if any components are missing. A much-quoted example of irreducible complexity is the bacterial flagellum, a minute propeller that moves certain bacteria. William Dembski, a mathematician, has sought a theoretical basis for naturally-occurring objects exhibiting **specified complexity**, in other words, being too complex to have arisen by natural processes alone. God is not openly identified as the intelligence, but appears to be implied.

Although the ID Movement is not exclusively anti-evolution, a misapplied argument for criticizing evolution is based on Fred Hoyle's analogy that a tornado blowing through a junkyard of Boeing 747 parts is unlikely to assemble a ready-to-fly 747. Similarly, it is claimed, a fully-working biological system is unlikely to arise suddenly from many highly improbable events. But the 747, like the mousetrap, is not alive and neither of them can adapt. Neither offer realistic analogies with living systems and this is not how evolution works. Richard Dawkins' helpful Climbing Mount Improbable analogy makes this point. He compares reaching a precipitous mountain-top in one leap with attaining the summit by a series of small steps round the other, gently-sloping side. This way, he eloquently illustrates how the eye is thought to have evolved independently more than 40 times.

In addition to modifying earlier forms of the design argument, other ways of claiming design were possible. One, expressed by Malthus and favoured by Darwin, was that 'laws of nature' were designed and pointed to a Lawgiver. A modern 'candidate for an argument for design' is the Goldilocks effect (pp. 67–69).

Problems with the ID Movement

- No one knows whether a natural explanation will be found tomorrow: then, on ID reasoning, 'intelligence' seems to be no longer required. Claims made a decade ago that the development of blood-clotting processes and immune systems could not be accounted for by evolution are now seen as incorrect.

- It seems to overlook how intermediate components of evolutionary processes have different functions at different stages of the evolutionary process. Even the various parts of a mousetrap could be used for other purposes than catching mice; for example, the spring could keep a box-lid closed.

- If only what has specified complexity points to intelligence, what about the rest of creation which is also seen as God's planning?

- It is difficult to see ID as other than a contemporary version of the 'God-of-the-gaps'.

ID claims to be a scientific theory, but this is misleading since it postulates 'intelligence' – a metaphysical/religious concept – to account for a current absence of scientific explanations. So therefore it is inappropriate to include ID in science teaching; but equally well it is inappropriate, in good science education, to imply that the belief that the universe is designed by God is negated by science. The traditional concept of design remains unaffected by the quality of the ID Movement's arguments.

Attempts to introduce ID and ideas of a young Earth, referred to earlier (pp. 101–102), in the name of 'fairness' and 'teaching the controversy', sound admirable but appear misguided. Questions of whether evolution has occurred, and whether the Earth is young or old, are not considered as controversial by the vast majority of academics, religious and non-religious, *whose scientific expertise lies in the relevant disciplines*.

A Chancy Business

- 'I bumped into John by chance this morning,' said Karen when she returned from the shops.

- 'The universe can emerge out of nothing, without intervention, by chance,' writes Professor Peter Atkins.

In both these cases the words 'by chance' are used to deny plan or purpose. Using this meaning, Darwin said:

'I may say that the impossibility of conceiving that this grand and wondrous universe, with our conscious selves, arose through chance, seems to me the chief argument for the existence of God; but whether this is an argument of real value, I have never been able to decide.'

We may deny the *appearance* of a plan in random processes or chance events. But we are not in a position to deny the *existence* of a plan unless we have every relevant fact. Karen would have been wrong in thinking her encounter with John was unplanned if John liked her, knew she went shopping every Saturday morning and walked round town till he 'bumped into her'.

Although there are mathematical tests for random sequences, the difficulty of not being in the know surrounds

Chance or not?

- fcuidvlgvpdgjfrjilcolysmdapcbuud
Produced by repeatedly selecting single letters of the alphabet while blindfolded. Completely unplanned.

- jkdleuhitehaoarcedndohcwnicemiae
Constructed from the first letter of a common nursery rhyme, followed by every third letter. Only one letter, in each position, fits the planned sequence.

- uijtajtabatfoufodfajoafbtzadpef
Each letter in a simple sentence is replaced by the following letter in the alphabet to give a simple code. At the ends, z becomes a space and a space becomes a. Again, each letter is necessary in that position. (A cryptologist would have noted the frequency of 'f's and 'a's and started cracking the code.)

No one believing the sequences were unplanned would have wasted time looking for any significance. That is only worthwhile if there is a rational mind behind it and it is intelligible.

all judgments of randomness. A convenient way of obtaining a random set of digits is to go down a page of a telephone directory, taking the last digit from each entry. Should this sequence be regarded as unplanned?

A cosmic accident?

If the universe is accidental and matter is all there is, our brains too are accidents. So can our beliefs, including 'the universe is accidental', be relied on? We assume they can, but we could be deluded, with no means of knowing. Professor J.B.S. Haldane once wrote:

> '...if my mental processes are determined wholly by the motions of the atoms in my brain, I have no reason to suppose that my beliefs are true... And hence I have no reason for supposing my brain to be composed of atoms.'

He later published '*I repent an Error*' in which he said, 'very intelligent people hold beliefs contradictory to [mine]'. But, if these contradictory beliefs are determined wholly, there are still no grounds for knowing which is true! The retraction was defective. A thorough-going determinist has to face up to the fact that his belief in determinism carries the consequence that the belief in determinism is itself determined.

'Chance' and 'random' in science

These terms can have precise meanings in science, as distinct from popular usage:

> 'The biological meaning of chance is that mutations happen regardless of whether they will be useful to the species when they occur, or ever.'
>
> PROFESSOR THEODORE DOBZHANSKY

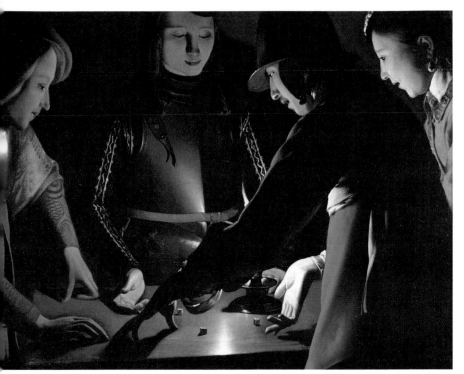

Confusion arises when a *popular* meaning of 'chance' ('unplanned') is applied to the word used in one of its *technical senses* (for example, 'unpredictable from prior data'); so too when a technical meaning ('species') is given to a word ('kinds') used in a popular sense (p. 15).

The Dice Players, by Georges de la Tour, 1650.

Unpredictability is involved in the above biological definition and in processes such as throwing dice, tossing coins, and radioactive decay.

Although such individual events are currently unpredictable, large numbers are highly predictable and law-like. As a former President of the Royal Society remarked, 'There are few laws more precise than those of perfect molecular chaos.' They indicate what to expect in long sequences, not in individual cases.

Chance and randomness plus selection play an important part in design. In addition to 'Darwinian design' or 'Evolution Strategy' being used to design efficient aerofoil sections, a much more sophisticated tool, **genetic algorithms**, has been invented. This mimics the biological processes of chance/random changes plus selection which result in adaptation in nature. It enables the exploration of huge numbers of potential solutions to a wide range of optimisation problems that would otherwise need unrealistic amounts of computing time. A recent application is to determine the best positioning of ambulances in particular areas.

If such biological analogies, employing chance/random changes plus selection, can be used by intelligent human agents to achieve desired goals, it can hardly be claimed that evolutionary processes are necessarily hostile to divine agency and purpose in nature. Evolution by natural selection does not remove the possibility of design; it changes its form.

Lady luck

'Chance' is sometimes used as though it were the *cause* of something happening:

> '... *chance is operating by causing these random changes, mutations, in the underlying genetic recipe.*'
> PROFESSOR RICHARD DAWKINS

Or even as a person – 'Lady Luck', who is able to think, plan and create – instead of simply a concept:

> '*Chance with natural selection, chance smeared out into innumerable tiny steps over aeons of time is powerful enough to manufacture miracles like dinosaurs and ourselves.*'
> PROFESSOR RICHARD DAWKINS

This way of speaking is sometimes called 'Tychism' after the Greek goddess of chance (although to be fair, Dawkins' recent book *The God Delusion* acknowledges 'the psychological bias that we all have towards personifying inanimate objects as agents').

> '*Sometimes chance led to a pattern... Sometimes chance patterned*

points into a space… the pattern chance stumbled upon crumbled… Then, by chance, there came about our fluctuation.'
PROFESSOR PETER ATKINS

It is misleading to talk about chance like this, even if only as a figure of speech. Personifying 'chance', even as a literary device, is not legitimate if the purpose of such usage is to press the thesis that science precludes God. Such use of the word degenerates into nonsense if a creating God is denied while a creating chance (plus natural selection) is affirmed.

'At first, as a convenient technical shorthand, he [the scientific secularist] embodies his ignorance in the notion of chance. But in his programme chance soon forgets her humble origins, and begins to play God. She becomes creative, and after much labour she gives birth, finally — to the scientific secularist!'
PROFESSOR DOUGLAS SPANNER

The oddity of treating 'chance' (absence of an identifiable cause) as though it were a person — the fallacy of reification (p. 103) — has been compared to treating 'nobody' (absence of a person) as though it were a person; as is done deliberately, for humour, in Lewis Carroll's *Alice Through the Looking Glass*:

'I see nobody on the road,' said Alice.
  'I only wish I had such eyes,' the King remarked in a fretful tone.
'To be able to see Nobody! And at that distance too!' 'Who did you pass on the road?' the King went on…
  'Nobody,' said the Messenger.
'Quite right' said the King, 'this young lady saw him too. So of course Nobody walks slower than you.'
  'I do my best,' the Messenger said in a sullen tone. 'I'm sure nobody walks much faster than I do!'
  'He can't do that', said the King, 'or else he'd have been here first.'

'…chance alone is at the source of every innovation, of all creation in the biosphere. Pure chance, absolutely free but blind, at the very root of the stupendous edifice of evolution…'

Professor Jacques Monod

Alice, the White King and the Rabbit Messenger. John Tenniel's illustration from the edition published in 1872.

The role of 'chance' processes in evolution has appeared in a new light following recent discoveries in biology. Far from life being an unlikely outcome of chance processes, one biologist, Professor Manfred Eigen, has argued:

> '... the evolution of life... must be considered an inevitable process despite its indeterminate course... it is not only inevitable "in principle" but also sufficiently probable within a realistic span of time'.

More recently Professor Simon Conway Morris, in his work on evolutionary convergence, reports that 'the evidence now strongly suggests humans to be an evolutionary inevitability'. The subtle interplay between 'chance' and 'law' seems to have played an important part in the living world being as it is.

A Created World

The book of Genesis opens on the positive note that the world is the work of a purposeful God. This book closes on a similar note.

Genesis was addressed to people who, like us, were constantly bombarded by contrary views about the origins and ownership of the world. It called for responsible management of Earth and its resources. This can be done to the glory of God or not, as was recognized in the second Charter of the Royal Society, where Fellows were commanded to direct their studies 'to the glory of God the Creator, and the advantage of the human race'.

Public opinion about science ranges between deifying and despising it. Some regarded science as the chief means

to peace and prosperity, and treated it as some kind of secular substitute for God. When the 'god' failed to deliver, they despised it. To abuse science because it fails to solve the world's ills is childish; comparable to the infant who kicks its toy because it will not do something for which it was never designed. Between these two extremes lies the rosy-spectacled view that, though science and technology have caused a lot of problems, they will also solve them.

Science and technology are fascinating activities. They make worthwhile careers. Professor Sir J.J. Thomson, associated with the discovery of the electron, wrote:

> '... in the distance tower still higher peaks, which will yield to those who ascend them still wider prospects, and deepen the feeling, the truth of which is emphasized by every advance in science, that "Great are the Works of the Lord".'

But we are imperfect people. Temptations to misuse and exploit for personal gain operate here as in every other department of life. But the answer to abuse is not disuse, but responsible use.

> 'Not until the power conferred by our knowledge has been recognized as God's gift, enabling his children to grow up into fully developed men and women... not until man's patient observation of the world around has led him on to awe and then to worship; not until our science has shown us with what rich lustre the heavens declare the glory of God, and the firmament shows his handiwork; not until then can human faith be as it was meant to be, nor human life fulfil its proper destiny; nor shall we see how all things are summed up in Christ, both things on earth and things in Heaven; and our hearts be so astonished at the splendour of God's creation that they grasp eternity in a moment of time, and are lost in wonder, love and praise.'
> PROFESSOR CHARLES COULSON

Endnotes

1 For a more detailed treatment see Lucas, E., *Can we believe Genesis today?*, (2nd ed.), Leicester: Inter-Varsity Press (2001).

2 Humphreys, C.J. 'The Star of Bethlehem', *Q Jl R astr. Soci.*, **32** 389–407 (1991); reprinted in *Science and Christian Belief*, **5** 83-101 (1993) www.cis.org.uk.

3 Humphreys, C.J. and Waddington, W.G. 'Dating the Crucifixion', *Nature*, **306** No. 5945, 743–46 (1983).

4 Humphreys, C.J. *The Miracles of Exodus*, HarperCollins, (2004).

5 Anderson, J.N.D., *The Evidence for the Resurrection*, Inter-Varsity Press.

6 'The Poole-Dawkins debate', available from Christians in Science [www.cis.org.uk].

7 'Metaphysics' – from the works of Aristotle written after (*meta*) his Physics. It is a term now used for first principles about the nature of ultimate reality, something that lies beyond the capability of science to address. It includes issues like mind-and-matter and facts-and-values.

Index

Picture Acknowledgments

p. 9 Stock Montage/Getty Images; p. 12 Stock Montage/Getty Images; p. 14 WorldFoto/Alamy; p. 16 Peter Horree/Alamy; p. 21 John Robertson/Alamy; p. 23 Michael Poole; p. 25 f1 online/Alamy; p. 27 The Print Collector/Alamy; p. 32 A. T. Willett/Alamy; p. 33 Michael Poole; p. 44 Elmtree Images/Alamy; p. 47 Matthew Dossett/Alamy; p. 49 Masanori Kobayashi/Alamy; p. 53 Visual Arts Library (London)/Alamy; p. 57 Nigel Hicks/Alamy; p. 59 The Print Collector/Alamy; p. 63 Douglas Hill/Beateworks/Corbis; p. 66 NASA; p. 72 The Print Collector/Alamy; p. 73 Visual Arts Library (London)/Alamy; p. 75 Mary Evans Picture Library/Alamy; p. 78 Visual Arts Library (London)/Alamy; p. 81 Mary Evans Picture Library/Alamy; p. 83 Gari Wyn Williams/Alamy; p. 92 JOCHEN LUEBKE/AFP/Getty Images; p. 93 Michael Poole; p. 95 Visual Arts Library (London)/Alamy; p. 96 Michael Poole; p. 97 Michael Poole; p. 98 The Print Collector/Alamy (both); p. 99 Michael Poole; p. 104 NORBERT MILLAUER/AFP/Getty Images; p. 110 Michael Poole; p. 112 Lion Hudson; p. 117 Imagno/Austrian Archives/Getty Images; p. 119 Mary Evans Picture Library/Alamy.